# Table of Contents

"May this Christmas bring us
Closer to the spirit of human understanding
Closer to the blessing of peace!"
-Author Unknown

# Holly Jolly Appetizers and Beverages

"The best of all gifts around any
Christmas tree: the presence of a happy
family all wrapped up in each other."

- Burton Hillis

# BACON-PECAN STUFFED MUSHROOMS

500 grams (1 pound) large fresh mushrooms
4 tablespoons butter
2 tablespoons canola oil
¼ teaspoon salt
2 tablespoons onion, finely chopped
1 cup soft bread crumbs
6 bacon strips, cooked and crumbled
2 tablespoons pecans, chopped
2 tablespoons sherry or beef broth
2 tablespoons sour cream
2 tablespoons chives, minced

Remove mushroom stems (discard). In large skillet, heat 2 tablespoons butter and oil over medium-high heat. Sauté mushroom caps for 2 minutes on each side; sprinkle with salt. Remove with a slotted spoon to paper towels. In the same skillet, sauté onion in remaining butter until tender. Remove from heat; stir in remaining ingredients. Spoon into mushroom caps. Place on a broiler pan; broil for 2-3 minutes or until filling is browned. Serve warm.

"Fatherhood is pretending the present
you love most Christmas morning is soap on a rope."
- Bill Cosby

# BRIE CHEESE APPETIZERS

Brie cheese has become very popular. We have discovered and tested some delicious Brie appetizer combinations. When you are using Brie, there are a few things to remember:

- White Brie rind is edible and is usually eaten along with the softer interior.
- If you do not want to eat the rind, it is easy to trim from refrigerated Brie or bring the cheese to room temperature, cut, and scoop out the soft centre with a spoon.
- Camembert may be substituted for Brie in equal measures, and is usually less expensive. Be aware that Camembert will be slightly stronger in aroma and flavour than Brie, but makes a very good substitution.
- Brie should be refrigerated and consumed within a few days.
- Brie may be frozen up to 6 months.
- Brie should be brought to room temperature or warmed before eating.
- Brie wheels come in different sizes — if a recipe calls for a large one, you may buy smaller ones, divide toppings among them and freeze the appetizer for use later.

*"Few things are more delightful*
*than grandchildren fighting over your lap."*
*- Doug Larson*

# CHUTNEY BAKED BRIE

1 -450 gram wheel Brie cheese

1 teaspoon ground curry powder

1 -200 ml jar mango chutney

2/3 cup cashews, chopped

1 French baguette, cut into ½ inch slices

Preheat oven to 350° F. Sprinkle curry powder over top and sides of Brie. Rub curry powder into rind to thoroughly coat surface. Place Brie wheel in a large pie plate or oven proof dish. Spread a generous layer of chutney over top, and evenly sprinkle with cashews. Bake 15 minutes in preheated oven, or until cashews are slightly golden and cheese inside rind is melted. Serve with slices of baguette.

# MUSHROOM BAKED BRIE

(A big hit on a cold night, serve warm with baguette slices.)

1 tablespoon butter

1 teaspoon garlic, crushed

2 tablespoons slivered almonds

1 -284 ml can sliced mushrooms, drained

1 tablespoon brandy

1 teaspoon dried tarragon

1 -226 gram wedge Brie cheese, coating removed

Preheat oven to 350° F. Melt butter in a medium saucepan over medium heat. Mix in garlic and almonds, heating until almonds are lightly browned. Stir in mushrooms and cook until tender, about 5 minutes. Add brandy and tarragon. Place Brie in a small baking dish. Pour mushroom and brandy mixture over Brie. Bake in preheated oven 20 minutes, or until bubbly.

# HOLIDAY BRIE
(It doesn't get any easier than this.)

½ cup sliced almonds
½ cup brown sugar
1 tablespoon Dijon mustard
1 -226 gram Brie cheese
1 loaf French baguette
vegetable oil spray

Coarsely chop ¼ cup of the almonds, and combine with sugar
and mustard. Mix well. Cut Brie in half horizontally. Place
one half of brie, cut side up, onto baking dish. Spread half of
sugar mixture evenly over bottom half of Brie. Top with
remaining half of Brie, cut side up. Spread remaining sugar
mixture over Brie, sprinkle with remaining almonds.
Cut baguette on a bias into ¼ inch thick slices. Arrange slices
around Brie; spray with oil. Bake at 425° F. for 8-10 minutes
or until baguette slices are golden brown and Brie begins to
soften. Remove from oven, let stand 5 minutes before serving.

*"The quality of my day can in turn affect the quality of someone
else's day. What it comes down to is this: You might be somebody's
only angel of the day. And you can't take that for granted."*
*- David Wagner*

4

# WARM SWEET PECAN TOPPED BRIE

1 -200 gram whole crème Brie
1 tablespoon brown sugar
1 tablespoon pecans, chopped
1 teaspoon butter, melted
berries or small butter cookies

With a long, sharp knife, cut off and discard the top rind of the cheese. Combine sugar, pecans and butter; mix well. Place Brie in an ovenproof container slightly larger than the cheese. Sprinkle mixture evenly over surface of cheese. Broil until cheese is soft, slightly melted and topping is bubbly. Serve warm with berries or cookies.

Apricot Topping:
Replace brown sugar, pecans and butter with ¼ cup apricot jam mixed with 2 teaspoons brandy. After removing top rind from cheese, prick surface with fork and pour 2 teaspoons brandy over all. Top with apricot mixture and bake 10 minutes in 350° F. oven. Sprinkle with toasted sliced almonds to serve.
Toppings can easily be doubled or tripled to cover 300 or 400 gram wheels of Brie or Camembert.

"Christmas waves a magic wand over this world, and behold, everything is softer and more beautiful."

- Norman Vincent Peale

# CANDY-APPLE DIP
### (Tastes just like a candy apple without the fuss.)

1 -250 gram package cream cheese, softened
½ cup brown sugar
½ cup caramel sauce
6 apples, cored and wedged
Beat softened cream cheese, add brown sugar and blend well.
Spread on a fancy plate or pie plate. Cover with caramel sauce.
Place apples in a bowl and serve.
Note: Dip apples in lemon juice or 7-Up to keep them from browning.

# ROQUEFORT GRAPES
450 grams Roquefort cheese, softened
2 -250 gram packages cream cheese, softened
450 grams seedless green grapes
450 grams pistachios, shelled
Combine Roquefort and cream cheese in bowl and beat until well blended. Wrap in waxed paper and refrigerate for at least 2 hours. Chill grapes at the same time. Place pistachios in a food processor and chop fine. Flatten pieces of cheese mixture with your hand and place a chilled grape in centre of mixture. Roll until grape is entirely coated and refrigerate again for about 3 hours. Remove grapes and roll in chopped pistachios. Arrange grapes and serve. You can also cut grapes in half.

**The only thing domestic about me is that I live indoors.**

# CARAMELIZED ONION DIP

2 large yellow onions (about 3 cups), chopped
4 tablespoons unsalted butter
¼ cup canola oil
½ teaspoon ground cayenne pepper
1 teaspoon salt
½ teaspoon pepper
½ cup cream cheese, at room temperature
½ cup sour cream
½ cup mayonnaise

Heat butter and oil in a large sauté pan over medium heat. Add onions, cayenne, salt, and pepper and sauté for 10 minutes. Reduce heat to medium-low and cook for 20 more minutes, stirring occasionally, until onions are browned and caramelized. Allow onions to cool, blot with paper towel. Mix cream cheese, sour cream and mayonnaise until well blended and smooth. Add onions and mix well. Serve at room temperature.

*"All values are important; everyone who has ever touched my life in some way was a mentor for good or bad. Life is a blend, and a person is a blend of all the influences that have touched their lives."*
*-General Colin Powell*

# CRAB CAKES
## (Quick and easy to make.)

1 egg

¼ cup ranch dressing

2 -170 gram cans crabmeat, drained and flaked

20 Ritz Crackers, coarsely crushed (about 1 cup)

1/3 cup 4-Cheese Italiano Shredded Cheese

2 green onions, chopped

¼ teaspoon cayenne pepper

Beat egg and dressing in large bowl with whisk until well blended. Stir in crabmeat. Add crackers, cheese, onions and pepper; mix well. Shape into 24 patties, using 1 tablespoon of the crab mixture for each. Place on baking sheet sprayed with cooking spray. Bake in a 375° F. oven for 5-7 minutes on each side until heated through.

# CRABMEAT DIP
## (Grated egg makes this an interesting dip.)

1 -120 gram can crabmeat, drained and flaked

½ cup mayonnaise

¼ cup cocktail sauce

2 tablespoons onion flakes or onion, finely chopped

2 hard-boiled eggs, finely grated

salt and pepper to taste

Mix together and chill well. Serve with crackers.

# EASY MUSHROOM CAPS

24 large mushrooms
2 -200 gram packages of Boursin cheese
Parmesan cheese

Remove stems. Fill caps with Boursin cheese. Sprinkle with Parmesan. Bake for about 30 minutes at 350° F. until mushrooms are tender and golden.

# HAM SALAD SPREAD

2 small cans flakes of ham
1 hard-boiled egg, chopped
2 tablespoons celery, finely chopped
2 teaspoons onion, finely chopped
2 teaspoons sweet pickle relish
¾ cup mayonnaise
1 tablespoon prepared mustard
assorted crackers

In a bowl, combine first five ingredients. Combine mayonnaise and mustard; add to ham mixture and mix well. Refrigerate until serving. Serve with crackers.

"Probably the reason we all go so haywire at Christmas time with the endless unrestrained and often silly buying of gifts is that we don't quite know how to put our love into words."--Harlan Miller

9

# HEARTY HOLIDAY HUMMUS
## (A quick, tasty and nutritious snack)

1 -540 ml can of garbanzo beans or chick peas, drained
1 clove garlic, crushed
2 teaspoons ground cumin
½ teaspoon salt
2 tablespoons lemon juice
3 tablespoons olive oil
3 tablespoons hot water

Blend all ingredients until a smooth paste. Scrape and pour into a serving dish. Let stand tightly covered in refrigerator for at least 30 minutes before serving. Excellent with bread sticks, pita or crackers.

# TACO TARTLETS

1 pound hamburger
2 tablespoons taco seasoning mix
2 tablespoons water
1 cup sour cream
2 tablespoons taco sauce
2 tablespoons olives, chopped
1 cup tortilla chips, crushed
½ cup Cheddar cheese, shredded

Combine hamburger, taco mix and water. Press into bottom and sides of greased tiny tart pans. Mix together: cream, taco sauce, olives and ¾ cup chips. Fill hamburger shells with mixture and top with mixed ¼ cup chips and cheese. Bake at 375° F. for 10 minutes. Serve with taco sauce or salsa.

# KRAUT SAUSAGE BALLS

1 pound fresh pork sausage
¼ cup onion, minced
1 ½ cups sauerkraut, drained, rinsed and snipped
2 tablespoons bread crumbs
canola oil
½ cup cream cheese
1 teaspoon prepared mustard
sprinkle of garlic salt
¼ cup flour
2 eggs
¼ cup milk
¾ cup bread crumbs

Crumble and cook sausage and onion until browned. Drain.
Mix in sauerkraut, 2 tablespoons bread crumbs, cheese, mustard
and garlic. Refrigerate until cool. Shape into 1 inch balls and
coat with flour. Combine egg and milk. Coat floured balls with
egg mixture and then in remaining bread crumbs. Deep fry at
400° F. until golden brown (approx. 2-3 minutes). These
can be cooked ahead of time and reheated for 10 minutes at
350° F.

"Perhaps the best Yuletide decoration

is being wreathed in smiles."

-Author Unknown

# POTATO SALAD BITES

10 small red potatoes
¼ cup pimiento-stuffed olives, chopped
2 teaspoons fresh parsley, minced
1 teaspoon onion, finely chopped
½ cup mayonnaise
1 ¾ teaspoons Dijon mustard
1/8 teaspoon pepper
¼ teaspoon salt
paprika
parsley sprigs, optional

Place potatoes in a large saucepan and cover with water. Bring to a boil. Reduce heat; cover and cook for 12-15 minutes or until tender. Drain and immediately place potatoes in ice water; drain and pat dry.
Peel two potatoes; finely dice and place in a small bowl. Cut remaining potatoes in half. With a melon baller, scoop out the pulp, leaving a thin shell; set shells aside. Dice pulp and add to the bowl. Stir in olives, parsley and onion. Combine mayonnaise, mustard, and pepper; gently stir into potato mixture. Sprinkle potato shells with salt; stuff with potato salad. Sprinkle with paprika. Chill for at least 1 hour before serving. Garnish with parsley if desired.

"Let's be naughty and save Santa the trip." -Gary Allan

# ROSEMARY CRANBERRY PECAN CRISPS
## (Try not to eat them all at once!)

2 cups flour
2 teaspoons baking soda
1 teaspoon salt
2 cups buttermilk
¼ cup brown sugar
¼ cup honey
1 cup dried cranberries
½ cup pecans, chopped
¼ cup sesame seeds
¼ cup flax seed, ground
1 tablespoon fresh rosemary

Preheat oven to 350° F. In a large bowl, stir together: flour, baking soda and salt. Add buttermilk, sugar, and honey and stir a few strokes. Add cranberries, pecans, sesame seeds, flax, and rosemary. Stir until just blended. Pour batter into two 4 x 8 inch greased loaf pans. Bake for about 45 minutes until golden and springy to the touch. Remove from pans and cool on a wire rack. The cooler the bread, the easier it is to slice really thin. You can leave it until the next day or pop it in the freezer. Slice the loaves as thin as you can and place slices in a single layer on an ungreased cookie sheet. Reduce oven heat to 300° F. and bake for about 15 minutes, then flip them over and bake for another 10 minutes, until crisp and deep golden.

13

# RUMAKI AND VARIATIONS

Rumaki is an hors d'oeuvre of mock-Polynesian origin. Its ingredients and method of preparation vary, but usually consists of water chestnuts, pieces of duck or chicken liver wrapped in bacon and marinated in soy sauce and either ginger or brown sugar. There are so many variations of this appetizer; it is amazing how many things taste wonderful wrapped in bacon. Here are a few we have tried:

## TRADITIONAL RUMAKI

12 slices bacon, halved crosswise
340 grams chicken livers, halved
12 whole water chestnuts, halved
¼ cup soy sauce
1 teaspoon fresh ginger, minced
2 tablespoons dry sherry
1 teaspoon sugar

<u>Marinade</u>: Combine soy sauce, ginger, sherry and sugar in a small bowl. Add chicken livers and water chestnut pieces and marinate in refrigerator for ½ hour. Place 1 chicken liver piece and 1 chestnut piece in centre of each bacon-half, wrap, and secure with a toothpick. Place on a broiler pan or shallow baking pan and broil, until bacon is crisp, about 10-15 minutes. Or, bake appetizers in a 375° F. oven for 20 to 25 minutes. Serve hot. Makes 24 appetizers.

# SHRIMP RUMAKI

1 pound medium shrimp, shelled (about 45)
½ teaspoon garlic powder
salt
15 slices bacon, cut crosswise into thirds

Sprinkle shrimp with garlic powder and a little salt. Wrap each shrimp in a piece of bacon and secure with toothpick. Arrange on a broiler rack. Broil for about 8-10 minutes, turning occasionally, until bacon is crisp and browned. Serve with cocktail picks.

# MUSHSROOM RUMAKI

15 slices of bacon, halved crosswise
30 medium white mushrooms, cleaned
¼ cup barbeque sauce (Cattleboys works great!)

Place 1 mushroom in centre of each bacon-half, wrap, and secure with a toothpick. Brush with barbeque sauce. Place on a broiler pan or shallow baking pan and broil until the bacon is crisp, about 10-15 minutes. Or, bake in a 375° F. oven for 20-25 minutes. Serve hot. Makes 30 appetizers.

"Christmas is a time when everybody wants his past forgotten and his present remembered."

- Phyllis Diller

# STUFFED PRUNE RUMAKI

½ cup cream cheese, softened
20 whole soft pitted prunes
10 slices of bacon, halved crosswise

Soften cheese and put into a ziplock bag. Seal open end of bag
and clip very tip of corner. Pry the prunes open and fill the
centre of prune with cheese. Wrap bacon loosely around prune
and fasten with toothpick. Bake at 375° F. for 20-25 minutes
or until bacon is crisp.

# SPINACH NUGGETS
(Tasty, make plenty, they freeze well. Skewer with cocktail picks
for easy handling. If you wish, serve with mustard sauce.)

2 -300 gram packages frozen spinach
2 cups of stove top dressing (not prepared)
1 cup Parmesan cheese, grated
dash ground nutmeg
6 eggs, beaten
½ cup butter, softened

Thaw spinach, squeeze out excess moisture. Combine with
remaining ingredients. Shape into walnut sizes balls. Bake at
350° F. for 10-15 minutes. Serve warm.

# SAVOURY CHEESEBALL

2 -250 gram packages of cream cheese
1 -250 gram Cheddar cold pack*
1 green pepper, chopped
1 red pepper, chopped
1 small white or red onion, chopped
½ cup pimento, chopped (or less, to taste)
1 tablespoon Worcestershire sauce
salt to taste
pepper to taste
walnuts, crushed
parsley, chopped fine

Soften cream cheese, and mix all the above ingredients except the last two. Roll in crushed walnuts and parsley before serving. Serve with crackers.
*Cheddar cold pack — MacLaren's Imperial Cold pack Cheddar cheese found in the cheese section in a container like sour cream.

"Wouldn't life be worth the living

Wouldn't dreams be coming true

If we kept the Christmas spirit,

All the whole year through?"

~ Author Unknown

# SESAME SALMON SPREAD

1 -250 gram package cream cheese, softened

2 tablespoons lemon juice

1 -213 gram can salmon, drained, bones and skin removed

¼ cup sour cream

1 garlic clove, minced

2 tablespoons sesame seeds

2 teaspoons Liquid Smoke, optional

1 teaspoon fresh cilantro, minced

1 teaspoon fresh parsley, minced

¼ teaspoon dried dill weed

¼ teaspoon salt

1/8 teaspoon pepper

assorted crackers

In a small bowl, beat cream cheese and lemon juice until fluffy.
Add the salmon, sour cream, garlic, sesame seeds, Liquid
Smoke, cilantro, parsley, dill, salt and pepper; beat until
combined. Cover and refrigerate for at least 2 hours. Serve
with crackers.

"Women complain about PMS, but I think of it as the
only time of the month when I can be myself."
- Roseanne Barr

# SWEET AND SAVOURY CHEESE SPREAD

1 -250 gram package cream cheese, softened
1 tablespoon onion, grated
1 teaspoon garlic, minced
¼ cup butter, cubed
¼ cup brown sugar, packed
1 teaspoon Worcestershire sauce
½ teaspoon prepared mustard
1 cup pecans, toasted and finely chopped
assorted crackers

In small bowl, mix cream cheese, onion and garlic. Transfer to a serving plate; shape into 6 inch disk or log. Set aside. In small pot, mix butter, brown sugar, Worcestershire and mustard. Cook and stir over medium heat for 4-5 minutes or until sugar is dissolved. Remove from heat; stir in pecans. Cool slightly. Spoon over cheese mixture. Serve with crackers. Serves 8.

"And the Grinch, with his Grinch-feet ice cold in the snow, stood puzzling and puzzling, how could it be so? It came without ribbons. It came without tags. It came without packages, boxes or bags. And he puzzled and puzzled 'till his puzzler was sore. Then the Grinch thought of something he hadn't before. What if Christmas, he thought, doesn't come from a store. What if Christmas, perhaps, means a little bit more." -Dr Seuss

# BUBBLY CRANBERRY PUNCH

2 cans jellied cranberry sauce
1 ½ cups orange juice
½ cup lemon juice
2 -1 litre bottles ginger ale, chilled
ice cubes

In a large pitcher or punch bowl, whisk the cranberry sauce until smooth. Whisk in orange and lemon juice. Just before serving, slowly stir in ginger ale. Add ice cubes.

# CHRISTMAS SLUSH PUNCH

2 ½ cups sugar
6 cups water ·
2 -4 serving size packages strawberry jelly powder
6 cups pineapple juice
2/3 cup lemon juice
4 cups orange juice
2 -2 litre bottles lemon-lime flavored carbonated beverage

In a large saucepan, combine sugar, water, and jelly powder. Boil for 3 minutes. Stir in pineapple juice, lemon juice, and orange juice. Divide mixture in half, and freeze in 2 separate containers. When ready to serve, place the frozen contents of one container in a punch bowl, and stir in 1 bottle of lemon-lime soda until slushy.

# CAPPUCCINO MIX
(Great to give as a gift; find a nice jar,
type out the directions and attach as a tag.
The recipient will remember you with every sip.)

1 cup instant chocolate powder mix (like Quick)
½ cup powdered coffee whitener
½ cup instant coffee granules
1 teaspoon skim milk powder
1 teaspoon ground cinnamon
¼ teaspoon ground nutmeg
If you are giving this as a gift, layer ingredients in order given in
a nice 2 ¼ - 2 ½ cup jar with a tight-fitting lid. If making for
your own use, mix ingredients and store in jar.
Directions:  Stir contents of jar before measuring. Measure 2
tablespoons powdered mix into blender. Add 1 cup boiling water.
Process until foamy. Sprinkle with nutmeg and serve.

# MOCHACCINO MIX
3 tablespoons powdered coffee whitener
1/3 cup sugar
¼ cup instant coffee granules
¼ cup cocoa (sifted if lumpy)
1 cup skim milk powder
Combine all ingredients in a 2 cup jar with a tight fitting lid.
Directions: Measure ¼ cup mix into blender. Add 1 cup hot
milk. Process until smooth and pour into mug. Top with whipped
cream. Sprinkle with grated chocolate or cinnamon. Serves 1.

21

# FOAMY SAUCE
(This sauce is great in coffee or served
on warm mincemeat pie or tarts.)

½ cup butter, softened

1 cup icing sugar

1 egg

1 package of Dream Whip, prepared /or tub of whipped topping

2 ounces Drambuie

Cream butter. Beat in icing sugar and egg. Set over hot water
and beat until smooth and light - about 7 minutes. Cool.
Fold in Dream Whip and Drambuie. Add a big scoop to your
favourite coffee and enjoy!

# MAPLE CINNAMON COFFEE
(Fancy coffee!)

6 tablespoons coffee (or to taste)

½ teaspoon ground cinnamon

½ cup maple syrup

4 ½ cups cold water

4 scoops whipped cream

sprinkle of ground cinnamon

Place coffee and ½ teaspoon cinnamon in filter of coffeemaker
brew basket. Pour syrup into empty carafe. Prepare coffee.
When brewing is complete, stir well. Pour into 4 large mugs.
Top with whipped cream and a sprinkle of cinnamon. Yummy!

# CRANBERRY MARTINI

1 ounce vodka
½ ounce orange liqueur
½ ounce dry vermouth
3 ounces cranberry juice
1 cup ice
cranberries for garnish

Combine vodka, orange liqueur, vermouth, cranberry juice, and ice in a cocktail shaker. Shake vigorously to chill. Pour into martini glasses, and serve. Garnish with cranberries.

# CINNAMON ORANGE CIDER

4 cups apple cider or juice
2 cups orange juice
3 tablespoons red-hot candies
1 ½ teaspoons whole allspice
4 ½ teaspoons honey

In a large saucepan, combine the cider, juice and candies. Place the allspice on a double thickness of cheesecloth; bring up corners of cloth and tie with string to form a bag. Add to pan. Bring to a boil. Reduce heat; cover and simmer for 5 minutes or until flavours are blended. Discard spice bag; stir in honey. Transfer to a slow cooker; keep warm over low heat.

# CRANBERRY APPLE CIDER
(This is not a sweet cider which some people prefer, you could however, add some brown sugar to taste.)

4 cups water
4 cups apple juice
1 ½ cups cranberries, fresh or frozen
1 orange, peeled and segmented
1 apple, cored, peeled and sliced
2 cinnamon sticks
Place all ingredients in slow cooker. Cover and cook on high for 30 minutes and then turn to low for up to 5 hours. Double or triple to fill slow cooker. If you're doubling the recipe, just add more water and apple juice. Enjoy!

# CRANBERRY FESTIVE PUNCH
(Refreshing, served hot or cold.)

4 cups cranberry juice
2 cups orange juice
1 cup pineapple juice
½ cup lemon juice
½ cup water
1/3 cup sugar
1 teaspoon almond extract
In a large container, combine all ingredients; stir until sugar is dissolved. Refrigerate until serving. Yield: 8 cups.

# CREAMY CRANBERRY SMOOTHIE

1 1/3 cups cranberry cocktail, chilled
3 cups frozen whole strawberries
3 bananas, cut up
1 1/3 cups plain or French vanilla yogurt
½ cup sugar
5 ½ cups cranberry cocktail, chilled
1/3 cup orange juice

Put first five ingredients in blender, and process until smooth. Pour into punch bowl. Add remaining cranberry cocktail and orange juice. Stir.

## ICE CREAM SLUSH
(This is a great creamy drink that is so easy because it is made up long before guests arrive!)

2 litres butterscotch ripple ice cream
2 litres pineapple juice
26 ounces Malibu rum
7-Up to Serve

Mix first three ingredients well and freeze for at least 24 hours. Scoop frozen ice mixture into a nice glass until ¾ full and fill with 7-Up. Serve with a spoon and straw.

**My mind works like lightning,
One brilliant flash and it is gone.**

25

# GLÜHWEIN
### (Glühwein is a warm, spicy, traditional German winter drink made from warmed wine.)

¾ cup water
¾ cup sugar
1 cinnamon stick
1 orange
10 whole cloves
1 -750 ml bottle red wine

In a saucepan, combine water, sugar and cinnamon stick. Bring to a boil, reduce heat and simmer. Cut orange in half and squeeze juice into simmering water. Push cloves into outside of orange peel and place peel into simmering water. Continue simmering for 30 minutes until thick and syrupy. Pour in wine and heat until steaming but not boiling. Remove clove-studded orange halves. Serve hot in mugs or glasses that have been preheated in warm water.

## MISTLETOE MARTINI
### (Great drink anywhere, but best under the mistletoe!)

1 ½ ounces Spiced Rum
½ ounce Baileys
2 ounces eggnog
Shake together with ice. Sprinkle nutmeg or cinnamon on top.

# MERRY MINT LIQUEUR
### (There will be merriment!)

¾ cup water

1 ½ cups sugar

1 tablespoon lime juice

1 ½ cups vodka

¼ teaspoon peppermint extract

1 ½ teaspoons vanilla

green food colour, few drops

Place water and sugar in a small saucepan. Bring to a boil, stirring until sugar dissolves. Reduce heat, cover and simmer for 20 minutes. Pour into a jar. Stir in remaining ingredients. Seal and store 1 month before using.

# WASSAIL
### (Great drink which fills the house with
### a sweet welcoming aroma.)

8 cups apple juice

4 cups cranberry juice

5 cinnamon sticks

2 teaspoons whole cloves

Combine all ingredients and simmer for 30 minutes. Serve hot!

### Recipes are like a dating service.
### They never end up looking like the picture.

# JOLLY GREEN SHOOTERS

3 ounces Crème de Cacao

3 ounces Crème de Menthe

¾ cup milk or cream

Blend together with ice. Serves 6 yummy shots! Cheers!

# PEPPERMINT HOT CHOCOLATE

(The best hot chocolate for the family and then add the schnapps
and you have a yummy adult drink when the kids go to bed.)

1/3 cup unsweetened cocoa powder

¾ cup sugar

1 pinch salt

1/3 cup boiling water

3 ½ cups milk

¾ teaspoon vanilla

4 ounces peppermint schnapps liqueur

½ cup light cream

4 peppermint candy canes

Combine cocoa, sugar and salt in a saucepan. Blend in boiling
water. Bring this mixture to an easy boil while you stir. Simmer
and stir for about 2 minutes. Watch that it doesn't scorch. Stir
in milk and heat until very hot, but do not boil! Remove from
heat and add vanilla. Divide between 4 mugs. Add schnapps
and cream to mugs of cocoa to cool to drinking temperature.
Serve in a Christmas mug with a candy cane as a stir stick!

# WAY BETTER THAN CARTON EGGNOG

4 cups milk (We use whole milk for Christmas!)
5 whole cloves
2 ½ teaspoons vanilla, divided
1 teaspoon ground cinnamon
12 egg yolks
1 ½ cups sugar
1 ½ - 2 cups light rum (depending on taste)
4 cups light cream
½ teaspoon ground nutmeg

Combine milk, cloves, ½ teaspoon vanilla, and cinnamon in a saucepan. Heat over low heat for 5 minutes and slowly bring milk mixture to a boil. In a large bowl, combine egg yolks and sugar. Whisk together until fluffy. Whisk hot milk and clove mixture slowly into the eggs. Pour mixture into saucepan. Cook over medium heat stirring constantly for 3 minutes or until thick. Do not allow mixture to boil. Stir to remove cloves and let cool for about an hour. Stir in rum, cream, remaining 2 teaspoons vanilla and nutmeg. Refrigerate overnight before serving.
*Leave out rum for family eggnog or to use in recipes.
*Good day to make a pavlova or some meringue kisses for the Christmas cookie tray with all those left-over whites.

"The trouble with talking too fast is you may
say something you haven't thought of yet."
- Ann Landers

29

# A Good Christmas

Our friend had only recently been informed that he was
born with one less than the usual number of ribs.
Laughing, he jested, "There's a helluva good woman out
there somewhere!" Visiting him at home in palliative care
was much easier because he chose to lighten things up
with his irrepressible sense of humour. Though visibly
fading he was a feisty soul.
His wife shared a glimpse of their last Christmas together.
Christmas that year was, as they say, the best of days and
the worst of days. It was a bittersweet Christmas. Our time
together was limited and more limiting due to the invading
cancer necessitating toxic medications that induced
periods of mental fog. We were determined to make the
best of the few precious moments of clarity.
Weeks before we had talked about death and dying, for
months prior, we hadn't. Death had been like the elephant
in the room. We dared to hope that through some miracle,
we wouldn't have to go there…. the last taboo. Thankfully
we didn't wait any longer and finally breached that reality.
In time, we chose to name them; the fears, the anxieties,
the hopes for the future and the ultimate life questions. We
grappled with issues in the here, and in the hereafter.
Believing seemed so effortless when life is smooth, but
when it gets rough we pray for firmer faith. All that we
had long believed came into sharp focus and was shaken
and tested with the anguishing reality of death at our door.
We could believe that this was the end, we're dead, we're
done, it's all over, life and death that's it. Or we could run
with the promises of the Christmas story, the historical and

faith event which we had mulled over since our childhood. We could step out in faith yet again and believe what we had long professed with our lips.

We chose the latter. It made all the difference.

Experiencing that Christmas with our four children snuggled around in that carefully decorated place was moving and memorable, even merry at times. The warm memories still bring us comfort these many years later. The transparent tenderness and love was demonstrated in some old, familiar ways and by bright, thoughtful new ways. This was the Christmas story lived in our circumstances. Love came to earth on that first Christmas and for our family on this very special Christmas, love and hope were real and present.

There was a touch, a word, laughter, and tears, new understandings, and forgiveness. Emotions were raw and exposed in the spilling of our deepest concerns and yearnings. It was a good Christmas, somehow healing and cathartic.

Although there was a pre-mortem loneliness, we made a conscious choice, we chose hope and thanksgiving that Christmas. Its legacy and the legacy of our husband and father, his prayer and our prayers would be to find the courage to live out these essential virtues, every Christmas and most importantly, day in and day out.

It was time to say goodbye, our family had learned that this hackneyed farewell word, is actually a contraction of an old Gaelic phrase which means "God be with ye." We believed in "good bye", from time into eternity.

We look forward to a good Christmas together again.

# A Christmas Tale

At this time of year it is patently clear
That the males are the ones who are blest.
Thoughts like "goodwill to men" we hear time and again
And we find them quite hard to digest.
As we women all know, men think they run the show,
And sometimes we allow them this pause.
But it gets on our nerves, like too many hors d'oeuvres
When we want to get at the main course.
Many times out of mind the same problem we find,
Leaving plans to the men folk is risky.
Christmas spirit they think is some kind of a drink,
Such as vodka, Bacardi, or whiskey.
Since we carry the load, men keep out of our road,
We are ready and willing and able.
For it's perfectly clear, that the stuffed turkeys here
Are not always confined to the table.
The traditional way is now rather passé,
Lets give credit, where credit is due.
Then you'll see, man or boy, in return you'll enjoy
The fruits of our goodwill to you.
.... Jacqueline Ramm

# Christmas Morning Brunches and Breads

"I wish we could put up some of the Christmas spirit in jars and open a jar of it every month."

- Harlan Miller

# HAM'N EGG MUFFET

6 slices of Black Forest ham, sliced in half
12 eggs
Cheddar cheese, grated (optional)
6 English muffins, toast, or bagels

Spray muffin tins with Pam. Place ham slices in muffin tins so they come up around sides. Break 1 egg into the centre of ham cup. Sprinkle with grated cheese. Bake at 350° F. for 20 minutes. Scoop out of muffin tins and put on muffin halves.

# DASHER'S EGG MUFFIN

12 eggs
1 cup cooked ham, finely diced
½ cup onion, chopped
¼ cup green pepper, chopped
¼ teaspoon salt
¼ teaspoon pepper
¼ teaspoon garlic powder
½ cup Cheddar cheese, shredded

Beat eggs; add remaining ingredients. Mix well. Spoon ⅓ cup of mixture into 12 lightly greased muffin cups. Bake at 350° F. for 20-25 minutes or until a knife inserted near the centre comes out clean.

# CHRISTMAS MORNING SKILLET
(An easy, filling, one-pan breakfast,
or supper, for a busy night.)

2 cups frozen shredded hash brown potatoes
1 cup fully cooked ham, diced
½ cup onion, chopped
2 tablespoons canola oil
6 eggs
salt and pepper to taste
1 cup Cheddar cheese, shredded
minced fresh chives for garnish

In a large skillet, sauté potatoes, ham and onion in oil for
10 minutes or until potatoes are tender. In a small bowl, beat
eggs, salt and pepper. Add to the skillet; cook stirring
occasionally until eggs are set. Remove from heat and gently stir
in cheese. Spoon onto a serving platter and sprinkle with chives.
Serves 4.

*"Grandchildren don't stay young forever, which is good*
*because Pop-pops have only so many horsey rides in them."*
*- Gene Perret*

# SPINACH CHEESE STRATA
(For a festive touch, garnish with red and green
pepper rings overlapped in the centre.)

½ cup onion, chopped

¼ cup sweet red pepper, chopped

¼ cup green pepper, chopped

2 tablespoons butter

1 -300 gram package frozen chopped spinach, thawed and
well drained

2 cups Wheat Chex

½ cup Cheddar cheese, shredded

½ cup Swiss cheese, shredded

6 eggs

2 cups milk

⅓ cup bacon, cooked and crumbled

1 teaspoon Dijon mustard

1 teaspoon salt

¼ teaspoon pepper

Preheat oven to 325° F. In a large skillet, sauté onion and
peppers in butter until crisp-tender. Remove from heat. Stir in
spinach and cereal. Spoon into greased 7 x 11 inch baking dish.
Sprinkle with cheeses. In a large bowl, combine eggs, milk,
bacon, mustard, salt and pepper. Pour over cheese. Bake for
45-50 minutes or until knife inserted near the centre comes out
clean. Let stand for 10 minutes before cutting.
Yield: 6-8 servings.

# CRAB QUICHE

3 large eggs
3 tablespoons flour
½ cup mayonnaise
½ cup light cream
¼ cup onion, minced

½ cup Swiss cheese, grated
½ cup Cheddar cheese, grated
16 ounces crabmeat, chopped
1 -9 inch pie shell, unbaked

Preheat oven to 350° F. In large bowl, mix eggs, flour, mayonnaise and cream until blended. Stir in onion and cheeses. Fold in crab. Pour into pie shell and bake for 45 minutes or until knife inserted in the centre comes out clean.

# STUFFING & EGG MUFFIN
(For a treat on a holiday morning try these easy, cheesy quiche-like cups.)

1 package chicken stuffing mix
8 eggs
2 tablespoons bacon bits
¼ cup Mozza-Cheddar shredded cheese

Prepare stuffing mix as directed on package. Press ¼ cup stuffing into bottom and up sides of 8 greased muffin cups, forming about ¼ inch rim around top of cup. Crack 1 egg into each stuffing cup. Sprinkle with bacon bits and cheese. Bake at 400° F. for 20 minutes, or until yolks are set. Let stand 5 minutes before serving. Serves 4-8.

# SAGE ONION QUICHE

2 large onions, thinly sliced
2 tablespoons butter
2 tablespoons fresh sage, minced
1 teaspoon fresh thyme, minced or ¼ teaspoon dried thyme
1 deep-dish unbaked pastry shell
1 cup Cheddar cheese, shredded
4 eggs
1 ½ cups evaporated milk
½ teaspoon salt
⅛ teaspoon pepper
⅛ teaspoon ground nutmeg

In a large skillet, sauté onions in butter until tender; drain. Stir in sage and thyme. Spoon into pastry shell. Sprinkle with cheese. In a bowl, whisk eggs, milk, salt, pepper and nutmeg. Pour over cheese. Bake at 425° F. for 15 minutes. Reduce heat to 375° F. Bake 20-25 minutes longer or until a knife inserted near the centre comes out clean. Let stand for 10 minutes before cutting. Yield: 6-8 servings.

"I stopped believing in Santa Claus when I was six.
Mother took me to see him in a department
store and he asked for my autograph."
- Shirley Temple

# CRUSTLESS VISITOR'S QUICHE
(Everyone will enjoy this healthy addition to the brunch buffet.)

½ cup light cream cheese
1 cup milk
4 eggs
¼ teaspoon pepper
1 -300 gram package frozen chopped spinach, thawed and squeezed dry
1 cup frozen chopped broccoli, thawed and well drained
1 small onion, finely chopped
3 cups Cheddar cheese, shredded
5 fresh mushrooms, sliced

In a small mixing bowl, beat cream cheese. Add milk, eggs and pepper, beat until smooth. Stir in spinach, broccoli, onion, Cheddar cheese and mushrooms. Transfer to a 10 inch quiche pan, coated with canola oil. Bake at 350° F. for 45-50 minutes, or until a knife inserted in the middle comes out clean.

*"A grandmother is a little bit parent,
a little bit teacher, and a little bit best friend."*
*- Author Unknown*

# SWEET ONION QUICHE
(This has become a real favourite even with
people who are not big onion fans!)

1 cup flour
¾ teaspoon salt, divided
½ cup plus 3 tablespoons butter, divided
½ cup small curd cottage cheese
3 large sweet onions, sliced (about 6 cups)
(Walla Walla onions work great!)
4 ounces Canadian bacon, diced
¼ teaspoon pepper
3 eggs, lightly beaten
1 cup Cheddar cheese, shredded

In a small bowl, combine flour and ¼ teaspoon salt. Cut in
½ cup butter until crumbly. Gradually add cottage cheese,
tossing with a fork until dough forms a ball. Roll out pastry to fit
a pie plate. (Dough is a bit sticky so it is helpful to roll between
wax or parchment paper.) Transfer pastry to pie plate. Trim and
flute edges. In large skillet, sauté onions in remaining butter until
golden brown. Stir in bacon, pepper and remaining salt. Remove
from heat; add eggs and Cheddar cheese. Pour into pastry
shell. Bake at 350° F. for 40-45 minutes or until a knife
inserted near the centre comes out clean. Cut into wedges and
serve with fruit.

# ITALIAN QUICHE

1 -318 gram tube refrigerated crescent rolls
1 large sweet red pepper, chopped
1 tablespoon olive oil
1 garlic clove, minced
5 eggs, beaten lightly
½ cup mozzarella cheese, shredded
½ cup frozen chopped spinach, thawed and squeezed dry
¼ cup sliced pepperoni, cut into strips
¼ cup light cream
2 tablespoons Parmesan cheese, grated
1 tablespoon fresh parsley, minced
1 tablespoon fresh or dried basil, minced
dash pepper

Separate crescent dough into eight triangles; place in an ungreased pie or fluted tart pan with points toward the centre. Press into the bottom and up the sides to form a crust; seal seams. In a small skillet sauté red pepper in oil until tender. Add garlic; cook 1 minute longer. Remove from heat. In another small bowl, combine remaining ingredients; stir in red pepper mixture. Pour into crust. Bake at 375° F. for 25-30 minutes or until a knife inserted near the centre comes out clean. Let stand for 5 minutes before cutting.

# HUGS AND QUICHES
(When they taste these quiches - the cook will receive hugs!)

1 pound bacon, cooked and broken into pieces
1 ½ cups green onion, finely chopped
½ red pepper, finely chopped
½ green pepper, finely chopped
700 grams (1 ½ pounds) fresh mushrooms, chopped
small bunch broccoli, chopped
6 eggs, beaten
1 ½ cups cream milk
5 tablespoons dill, chopped
salt and pepper to taste
4 dozen 3 inch tart shells
2 cups Cheddar cheese, shredded

Distribute combinations of bacon and vegetables as desired in tart shells. Examples: bacon and onion, green and red pepper, bacon and mushroom, mushroom and green onion. Mix eggs, milk, dill, salt and pepper. Pour mixture over ingredients in tart shells. Put a pinch of cheese on the top of each. Bake at 350° F. for 25-30 minutes. These freeze well; to warm, put in 325° F. oven for 12-15 minutes.

Option: 3 cans broken shrimp (instead of bacon).

"It is Christmas in the heart that puts Christmas in the air."
-W.T. EllisEijen

# BERRY BUTTERMILK SCONES
(Loaded with cranberries, a favourite for holiday brunches.)

3 cups flour
⅓ cup plus 2 tablespoons sugar
2 ½ teaspoons baking powder
¾ teaspoon salt
½ teaspoon baking soda
¾ cup cold butter or margarine
1 cup buttermilk
1 cup dried cranberries
1 teaspoon orange rind, grated
1 tablespoon milk
¼ teaspoon ground cinnamon

Combine flour, ⅓ cup sugar, baking powder, salt, and baking soda; cut in butter. Stir in buttermilk just until combined. Fold in cranberries and orange rind. Turn onto floured surface, divide dough in half. Shape each portion into ball and pat into 6 inch circle. Cut each circle into six wedges. Place on lightly greased baking sheet. Brush with milk. Combine cinnamon and remaining sugar; sprinkle over scones. Bake at 375° F. for 15-20 minutes or until golden brown.
Dried blueberries or raisins can be substituted for cranberries. These can be frozen. Warm up to serve.

**If you think you're too small to be effective;
you've never been in the dark with a mosquito.**

Shown on previous page:

Cream-Filled Cinnamon Coffee Cake — Page 46
Cinnamon Orange Cider — Page 23
Crustless Visitor's Quiche — Page 38
Fruit Salad — Page 106
Blueberry Lemon Brie Scones — Page 43
Way Better than Carton Eggnog — Page 29

# BLUEBERRY LEMON BRIE SCONES

1 egg

½ cup milk

¼ cup butter

1 teaspoon vanilla

¼ cup sugar

1 tablespoon lemon zest

1 ½ cups whole wheat flour

2 teaspoons baking powder

1 cup blueberries, fresh or frozen

1-450 gram wheel Brie cheese, sliced

Cover a cookie sheet with parchment paper. Beat egg and add milk, butter and vanilla. Set aside. In a large bowl, combine sugar, lemon zest, flour and baking powder and form a well in the middle. Pour liquid into the well and mix until blended. Add blueberries. Divide dough into 12 balls. Place on cookie sheet, flatten slightly. Bake 12-15 minutes at 425° F. or until scones are well browned. When scones are ready, split and insert a slice of Brie into each.

"Christmas is not as much about opening our presents as opening our hearts."
- Janice Maeditere

# BONUS SKIP-BREAKFAST COOKIE
(Nice addition to brunch or healthy Santa snack.)

1 cup whole wheat flour

1 teaspoon baking soda

¾ teaspoon salt

½ teaspoon allspice

2 teaspoons ground cinnamon

1 ½ teaspoons ground ginger

2 eggs

⅓ cup canola oil

1 ¼ cups unsweetened applesauce

¾ cup brown sugar

1 tablespoon orange rind, grated

2 teaspoons vanilla

2 ½ cups oatmeal

½ cup flax, ground or whole

¾ cup almonds, chopped

½ cup sunflower seeds

1 cup raisins, (dried cranberries or blueberries also work well)

Combine first 6 ingredients in a bowl, stir well. Place eggs, oil, applesauce, and brown sugar in a large bowl, beat together well. Mix in dry ingredients. Add orange rind, vanilla, oatmeal, flax, almonds, sunflower seeds and raisins, stir until well blended. Using large spoon, portion out cookie dough and drop onto a greased cookie sheet, and press into a circle. Bake at 350° F. for 15-20 minutes. Cool. These freeze well.

# COCOA BANANA CRUNCH CAKE
## (Great with coffee, for brunch or anytime!)

½ cup butter, softened
½ cup sugar
1 cup ripe bananas, mashed
2 egg whites, slightly beaten
1 teaspoon vanilla
1 cup flour
⅔ cup oatmeal
⅓ cup cocoa
¼ teaspoon salt
1 teaspoon baking soda

Topping:
⅔ cup oatmeal
⅓ cup brown sugar
2 tablespoons butter, melted
½ teaspoon ground cinnamon

Beat butter and sugar, blend in banana, egg whites and vanilla. Add combined flour, oats, cocoa, salt and baking soda. Mix well. Spread in 8 inch square, greased pan. Combine topping ingredients and spread over bottom mixture. Bake at 350° F. for about 30-35 minutes.

# CREAM-FILLED CINNAMON COFFEE CAKE
(Great to make ahead and refrigerate, or
welcome company with its fresh-baked aroma.)

½ cup butter, softened

1 cup sugar

2 eggs

1 teaspoon vanilla

1 ½ cups flour

½ teaspoon baking soda

½ teaspoon salt

1 cup sour cream

Topping:

½ cup sugar

½ cup pecans, chopped

2 teaspoons ground cinnamon

Filling:

1 tablespoon cornstarch

¾ cup milk

¼ cup butter, softened

¼ cup shortening

½ cup sugar

½ teaspoon vanilla

Continued next page........

# CREAM-FILLED CINNAMON COFFEE CAKE

continued.........

Preheat oven to 350° F. In a large bowl, cream butter and sugar until light and fluffy. Add eggs, one at a time, beating well after each addition. Beat in vanilla. Combine the flour, baking soda and salt; add to creamed mixture alternately with sour cream, beating just until combined. Pour into two greased and waxed paper-lined 9 inch round baking pans. Combine the topping ingredients; sprinkle over batter. Lightly cut through with a knife to swirl. Bake for 20-25 minutes or until a toothpick comes out clean. Cool for 10 minutes; remove from pans to wire racks to cool completely. In a small saucepan, combine cornstarch and milk until smooth. Bring to a boil; cook and stir for 1-2 minutes or until thickened. Cover and refrigerate until chilled. In a small bowl, cream butter, shortening and sugar until light and fluffy. Add vanilla and chilled milk mixture; beat on medium speed until smooth and creamy, about 10 minutes. Place one cake on a serving plate; spread with filling. Top with remaining cake. Store in refrigerator. Yield: 8-10 servings.

"Personally I stay away from natural foods. At my age I need all the preservatives I can get."
- George Burns

# CRANBERRY COFFEE CAKE
## (A great quick bread.)

2 cups biscuit baking mix
2 tablespoons sugar
⅔ cup milk
1 egg, lightly beaten
⅔ cup jellied cranberry sauce

Topping:
½ cup walnuts, chopped
½ cup brown sugar, packed
½ teaspoon ground cinnamon

Glaze:
1 cup icing sugar
2 tablespoons milk
¼ teaspoon vanilla

Preheat oven to 400° F. In a large bowl, combine biscuit mix, sugar, milk and egg. Pour into a greased 8 inch square baking dish. Drop cranberry sauce by teaspoonfuls over batter. Combine topping ingredients; sprinkle over cranberry sauce. Bake for 18-23 minutes or until golden brown. Cool on a wire rack. In a small bowl, combine glaze ingredients; drizzle over coffee cake. Yield: 9 servings.

# OVERNIGHT COFFEE CAKE
(If you happen to have a menopausal moment this can be successfully baked 2 days later.)

⅓ cup margarine, softened

½ cup sugar

¼ cup brown sugar

1 egg, beaten

1 cup flour

½ teaspoon baking powder

¼ teaspoon baking soda

½ teaspoon ground cinnamon

½ cup buttermilk

¼ cup brown sugar

¼ cup pecans

¼ teaspoon ground cinnamon

⅛ teaspoon ground nutmeg

Cream margarine and sugars together. Add egg; mix well. Mix flour, baking powder, baking soda and cinnamon and add to creamed mixture alternately with buttermilk. Beat well. Spread into a greased 8 inch pan. Mix sugar, pecans, cinnamon and nutmeg and sprinkle over batter. Cover and refrigerate overnight. The next morning, remove from refrigerator and let sit for 15 minutes. Bake at 350° F. for 40-45 minutes or until a toothpick comes out clean.

# OATMEAL MOLASSES PANCAKES

2 eggs, beaten
2 cups buttermilk
1 cup oatmeal
1 tablespoon molasses
1 tablespoon canola oil
1 cup flour
1 teaspoon baking soda
1 teaspoon baking powder
½ teaspoon salt

In large bowl, mix eggs and buttermilk. Add oatmeal and mix well. Stir in molasses and oil. Add flour, baking soda, baking powder and salt. Add more milk if batter becomes too thick. Heat griddle, pour or scoop batter onto the griddle, using approximately ¼ cup for each pancake. Brown on both sides and serve hot.

*"To a small child, the perfect granddad is unafraid of big dogs and fierce storms but absolutely terrified of the word "boo."*
*- Robert Brault*

# SNOW LIGHT WAFFLES
## (Light and delicious, Mrs. Claus' favourite, great with Rudolph's Red Sauce.)

1 ⅔ cups flour
2 tablespoons sugar
1 tablespoon baking powder
¾ teaspoon salt
1 ¾ cups milk
2 eggs, separated
⅓ cup butter or margarine, melted

Mix together in a medium sized bowl; flour, sugar, baking powder, and salt. Stir in milk, egg yolks and butter, beat until smooth.
Beat egg whites until soft peaks form, fold into batter. Pour enough batter into hot greased waffle iron and spread within 1 inch of edge. Bake until steaming subsides and waffle is golden, 4-5 minutes. Serve immediately with your favourite topping.

# RUDOLPH'S RED SAUCE

1 -540 ml can cherry pie filling
1 cup jellied cranberry sauce
¼ cup maple syrup
¼ cup orange juice
3 tablespoons butter
Place all ingredients in a sauce pan and bring to a boil, turn down and simmer for 2 minutes. Serve warm over waffles.

# OVERNIGHT CINNAMON FRENCH STRATA

2 tablespoons butter
5 Golden Delicious apples, peeled and sliced
⅓ cup brown sugar
3 tablespoons apple juice or water
1 loaf cinnamon/raisin bread
2 ½ cups milk
½ teaspoon ground cinnamon
8 eggs
1 tablespoon butter
2 tablespoons sugar

Melt 2 tablespoons butter in skillet and cook apples about 20 minutes until golden. Add apple juice (water) and sugar during the last minute. Grease 9 x 13 inch baking pan. Arrange ½ of bread slices in pan, overlapping slightly. Blend milk, cinnamon and eggs. Pour half of egg mixture over bread. Spread ¾ of apple mixture over bread/egg layer evenly. Place remaining bread over apples, and then pour remaining egg mixture over that. Press bread gently, to help it absorb egg mixture. Melt the 1 tablespoon of butter, pour over bread mixture and sprinkle with sugar. Cover and chill overnight. Bake the next day at 325° F. uncovered for 50-55 minutes or until knife comes out clean. Reheat reserved ¼ of apple mixture and spoon over the top of the French toast as served.

# EGG SALAD BREAKFAST MUFFINS
(Four bagels can be substituted for
the English muffins; do not toast.)

6 eggs, hard-boiled, chopped
½ cup salad dressing
2 tablespoons sweet pickle relish
¼ teaspoon prepared mustard
4 English muffins, split, toasted
8 slices bacon, cooked (or ham)
½ cup Cheddar cheese, shredded

In small bowl, combine eggs, salad dressing, relish and mustard; blend well. Top each toasted muffin half with a slice of bacon or ham. Top with about ¼ cup of egg mixture. Place on ungreased cookie sheet; sprinkle each with 1 tablespoon cheese. Bake in 350° F. oven for 6-8 minutes or until thoroughly heated and cheese is melted. Makes 8.

**I love you more than yesterday.
Yesterday you really got on my nerves!**

"I once bought my kids a set of batteries for Christmas
with a note on it saying, toys not included."
- Bernard Manning

# BRAN MUFFINS
### (Wholesome, and tasty for your holiday brunch buffet)

4 cups flour
4 cups bran
1 ¾ cups white sugar
2 heaping teaspoons baking powder
2 heaping teaspoons baking soda
1 teaspoon salt
2 cups raisins
2 cups orange juice
2 cups cold milk
2 cups canola oil
2 teaspoons vanilla
5 eggs, beaten

Mix dry ingredients well. Add liquids and eggs. Stir and let stand 5 hours. Place in greased or lined muffin cups and bake for 20 minutes at 350° F. Serve warm with butter or jam on Christmas morning.
This is a large recipe that freezes well.

**Pity the people who have no opinion, for they shall go through life without a bumper sticker.**

# CINNAMON APPLE MUFFINS
### (The cinnamon-honey butter is a tasty accompaniment.)

1 ½ cups flour
½ cup sugar
1 ¾ teaspoons baking powder
½ teaspoon salt
½ teaspoon ground cinnamon
⅛ teaspoon ground nutmeg
1 egg
½ cup milk
3 tablespoons canola oil
3 tablespoons unsweetened applesauce
1 medium apple, peeled and grated

Topping:
¼ cup brown sugar, packed
1 tablespoon flour
2 tablespoons butter, cold
½ cup quick cooking oats

Cinnamon-Honey Butter:
½ cup butter, softened
¼ cup honey
½ teaspoon cinnamon

Preheat oven to 350° F. In a large bowl, combine flour, sugar, baking powder, salt, cinnamon and nutmeg. In another bowl, whisk the egg, milk, oil and applesauce. Stir into dry ingredients just until moistened. Fold in apple. Fill greased or paper-lined muffin cups half full.

For topping; in a small bowl, combine brown sugar and flour; cut in butter until crumbly. Add oats. Sprinkle over muffins. Bake for 18-22 minutes or until a toothpick inserted near the centre comes out clean. Cool for 5 minutes before removing from pan to a wire rack.

In a small bowl, beat the butter, honey and cinnamon until blended. Serve with warm muffins. Refrigerate leftover butter. Yield: 1 dozen.

# SWEET CORN MUFFINS

(Try these delicious muffins; they can be served
with a main dish, brunch or just a good snack.)

½ cup butter

⅔ cup sugar

¼ cup liquid honey

2 eggs

½ teaspoon salt

¾ cup yellow cornmeal

1 ½ cups flour

½ teaspoon baking powder

½ cup milk

¾ cup frozen corn

In a large bowl, cream together: butter, sugar, honey, eggs and salt. Add cornmeal, flour and baking powder; blend thoroughly. Add milk while mixing. Add corn to mixture and combine by hand until corn is mixed in. Grease 12 cup muffin tin and fill each cup with batter. Bake at 400° F. for 20-25 minutes or until muffins begin to brown on top.

Tact is the ability to close your mouth
before someone else wants to.

# GINGERBREAD MUFFINS
(This batter may be stored for several weeks in the refrigerator.)

1 cup shortening

1 cup sugar

1 cup molasses

4 eggs

2 teaspoons baking soda

1 cup buttermilk

4 cups flour

2 teaspoons ground ginger

½ teaspoon ground cinnamon

½ teaspoon ground cloves

½ cup pecans, chopped

1 cup raisins

In a mixing bowl, cream shortening and sugar until light and fluffy. Stir in molasses; then add eggs one at a time beating well after each. Dissolve baking soda in a cup with buttermilk. In a separate bowl combine flour with spices and add to creamed mixture alternately with buttermilk. Stir in pecans and raisins. Store batter in an air-tight container in refrigerator. When ready to bake, fill greased muffin cups ⅔ full. Bake at 350° F. for about 20 minutes or until done. To bake room temperature batter, reduce baking time to 15 minutes. Makes about 6 dozen muffins.

# DATE BRAN MUFFINS
## (Low fat and delicious!)

3 eggs

1 ½ cups applesauce

4 bananas, mashed

½ cup skim milk

1 cup brown sugar

¾ cup sugar

¼ cup molasses

1 teaspoon vanilla

3 cups bran

3 teaspoons baking powder

3 teaspoons baking soda

1 teaspoon salt

3 cups flour

1 cup raisins

1 cup dates, chopped

Beat eggs, add applesauce, bananas, milk and sugars. Mix in molasses, vanilla and bran. Add baking powder, baking soda, salt, and flour. Stir in raisins and dates. Bake at 350° F. for about 20 minutes.

Yields: 24 muffins.

*"If we can conquer space we can conquer world hunger."*
*- Buzz Aldrin*

58

# ORANGE BLUEBERRY MUFFINS

1 cup oatmeal

1 ½ cups orange juice

1 cup whole wheat flour

2 cups white flour

4 teaspoons baking powder

½ teaspoon baking soda

⅔ cup sugar

⅓ cup Splenda

1 cup canola oil

3 eggs, beaten

1 ½ cups blueberries, fresh or frozen

1 tablespoon orange zest, grated

Topping:

½ cup walnuts, finely chopped

⅓ cup sugar

1 teaspoon ground cinnamon

Combine oatmeal and orange juice and set aside. In a large mixing bowl, combine flours, baking powder, baking soda and sugars. Make a well in the centre of dry ingredients and add oatmeal mixture, oil and eggs. Stir only until ingredients are moistened. Carefully fold in berries and orange zest. Spoon batter into greased or paper-lined muffin tins, filling to about ¾ full. Combine walnuts, sugar and cinnamon. Sprinkle over muffins and bake at 400° F. for 15 minutes or until muffins test done.

# CHRISTMAS EGGNOG CHERRY LOAF

½ cup red or green maraschino cherries, chopped
½ cup walnuts or pecans, chopped
2 ½ cups flour, divided
¾ cup sugar
1 tablespoon baking powder
1 teaspoon salt
1 egg, beaten
1 ¼ cups eggnog
⅓ cup canola oil

Toss cherries and nuts in ½ cup of flour coating them well. In a small bowl stir together: remaining 2 cups flour, sugar, baking powder and salt. Mix egg, eggnog and oil into a separate mixing bowl. Stir in dry ingredients, mixing well. Add nut and cherry mixture. Mix and pour into a greased and floured 4 x 8 inch loaf pan. Bake at 350° F. for 40-50 minutes or until a toothpick comes out clean. Cool for 10 minutes before removing from pans.

"The best baby-sitters, of course, are the baby's grandparents. You feel completely comfortable entrusting your baby to them for long periods, which is why most grandparents flee to Florida."
- Dave Barry

# MOLASSES DATE LOAF

½ cup flour
1 teaspoon baking powder
1 teaspoon baking soda
pinch of salt
2 cups flour
4 tablespoons butter, melted
1 ½ cups sour milk or buttermilk
½ cup molasses
1 cup dates, chopped
1 cup pecans, chopped

Preheat oven to 375° F. Combine dry ingredients. Stir in butter, milk and molasses. Add dates and pecans. Lightly grease a 4 x 8 inch loaf pan. Let batter sit for 20 minutes prior to baking. Bake for 40-50 minutes.

"One good thing about snow - it makes your lawn look as good as your neighbour's."
- Clyde Moore

# MINCEMEAT FRUIT LOAF
### (Quick and easy, a must-try delicious moist loaf.)

2 ½ cups flour
1 teaspoon baking soda
1 cup glace cherries
2 cups glace fruit mix
1 cup pecan halves
2 eggs, beaten
1 can sweetened condensed milk
3 cups mincemeat

In large bowl mix together flour and baking soda. Add fruit and nuts; blend well. Add eggs, condensed milk and mincemeat. Mix well. Put into two 4 x 8 inch well-greased loaf pans. Bake at 250° F. for approximately 3 hours and 15 minutes. Let cool in pans for about 30 minutes before removing. (Baking times will vary depending on the size of your loaf pans, you could use 3 smaller ones and bake for 3 hours.) Hint: Place a pan, half filled with water, on the bottom rack of the oven while baking - makes for a moister cake.

*Each day comes bearing its gifts.*
*Our part is to untie the ribbons.*

# PUMPKIN LOAF

3 ½ cups flour
1 cup brown sugar
2 teaspoons baking soda
1 teaspoon baking powder
¾ teaspoon salt
1 teaspoon ground cinnamon
½ teaspoon ground cloves
1 egg
2 cups cranberry sauce
1 ¾ cups pumpkin purée
½ cup canola oil
1 tablespoon orange zest, grated
2 tablespoons walnuts, chopped

Preheat oven to 350° F. Combine flour, brown sugar, baking soda, baking powder, salt, cinnamon and cloves in large bowl and set aside. Mix egg, cranberry sauce, pumpkin, oil and orange zest. Mix together with flour mixture. Add walnuts. Pour into two greased 4 x 8 inch loaf pans. Bake 55-60 minutes or until a toothpick comes out clean.

"Blessed is the season which engages the whole
world in a conspiracy of love!"
- Hamilton Wright Mabie

# BUTTERSCOTCH BREAD

1 egg, beaten
1 cup brown sugar
2 tablespoons butter, melted
2 cups flour
½ teaspoon baking soda
1 teaspoon baking powder
¼ teaspoon salt
1 cup sour milk or buttermilk
½ cup raisins
½ cup nuts, chopped (use pecans or almonds or combination)

Preheat oven to 350° F. Combine egg, sugar, and butter. Beat well. Add flour and the rest of the dry ingredients alternately with milk. Add raisins and nuts. Pour into a lightly greased 4 x 8 inch loaf pan. Let batter sit for 20 minutes prior to baking. Bake for 45 minutes.

"My grandkids believe I'm the oldest thing in
the world. And after two or three hours
with them, I believe it, too."
- Gene Perret

# IRISH BREAD

1 ½ cups flour
1 ½ teaspoons baking powder
pinch of salt
½ cup sugar
¼ cup butter
½ cup milk
1 egg, beaten
1 cup raisins
1 teaspoon caraway seed

Preheat oven to 350° F. In a large bowl combine dry ingredients. Cut in butter as you would for pastry. Add the milk and beaten egg. Add raisins and caraway seed. Grease cookie sheet. Form dough into a circular mound. Bake for 30-35 minutes. Cut in wedges to serve.

*"Becoming a grandmother is wonderful.*
*One moment you're just a mother.*
*The next you are all-wise and prehistoric."*
*-Pam Brown*

# CINNAMON BUNS
## (These are the best cinnamon buns you'll ever taste!)

4 eggs
½ cup sugar
½ cup canola oil
3 ½ cups warm water
1 ½ teaspoons salt
2 tablespoons Quick Rising Yeast
8-10 cups flour

1 ⅓ cups brown sugar
½ cup butter, melted
2 teaspoons ground cinnamon
⅔ cup raisins

Beat eggs, add sugar and oil. Add water, salt and yeast. Mix in flour 1 cup at a time. Finish by kneading dough until smooth. Let rise for 1 hour.
Mix brown sugar, butter, cinnamon and raisins. Roll out half of the dough at a time. Spread each half with half the cinnamon mixture. Roll up and cut into 1 inch slices. Place on a greased pan. Let rise until doubled in size. Bake at 350° F. for 20-25 minutes.

**My next house will have no kitchen
- just vending machines and a large trash can.**

# REINDEER ON MY ROOF

My parents sat on the fence, Christmas was Jesus' birthday, but Santa ... well... they wouldn't give me a straight answer when I questioned them whether or not he was real. Besides, they were mostly preoccupied. I grew up in a rambling farm home, number eleven out of thirteen children.

My Dad, in his heavy Flemish accent would grin and comment unabashedly to whomever would listen, "We have 'terteen' children!" The pre-Christmas or Advent season was filled with happy anticipation, concerts, work and clandestine activities.

I longed, however, to share in the excitement of my friends who believed in Santa Claus. Their behavior seemed to noticeably improve as Christmas drew near. They'd compare their elaborately decorated stockings and brag how each year Santa would fill those stockings with lavish and luscious treasures. I was somewhat envious. Oh, we received gifts alright, my older siblings would hand them out pathetically pretending to be Santa.

There was a certain protocol; for months we would stash away meager savings and then purchase a small gift for everyone, maybe just a coveted candy bar. My multiplication skills were limited but I figured there would be close to 200 gifts just within the family, so it was quite exciting. But how I longed to make my very own list for Santa, put up a stocking and have him pay a visit to our home.

Mama insisted that we could all be Santa and have the spirit of St. Nicholas, a spirit of love and giving. Mama seemed to know everything.... Christmas morning would arrive, after attending early church some miles away, we gulped down a hurried breakfast. Impatiently eager, but politely trying to remember our manners, we ripped open each gift in turn, as the mound of gifts stacked in front of the fireplace too quickly dwindled.

In my long seven years, disappointingly, there hadn't ever been a gift from Santa Claus.

That Christmas eve I lay pondering the wonder of the season. The night was clear, calm and lovely, the moon beamed through my frost-etched second story window. I felt warmly nostalgic, as I snuggled closer to my older sister. I had heard my brothers softly scheming between chores. I wondered what they were up to, maybe manufacturing some special surprise. The poem, "The Night Before Christmas" resonated in my head, I loved it and had it practically memorized. Reciting poetry was a staple of our rural education.

If Santa did arrive, he needed to be really cautious on our steep roofed, three story home. I hoped our chimney was unclogged. While musing on the logistics of a hypothetical visit from the jolly old elf, I thought I heard sleigh bells. Yes! I bolted wildly out of bed, waking my sister, yes there were bells! Sleigh bells! Was that, "the prancing and pawing of those little hoofs?" Were there reindeer on my roof?" Straining, I heard a faint "HO, HO, HO", I was ecstatic! Santa and his reindeer were here!

To my sheer delight, on Christmas morning, there was the most beautiful little doll for me, under the tree. The writing on the homemade tag looked mysterious and comforting. I quickly discounted the vague similarity to my brother Clifford's script. I couldn't wait to disclose every merry detail to my friends.

Fifty years and many festive feasts later have left me with a much wider girth and graying hair comparable to Ms. Claus. I'm older now and supposedly wiser. Mama's words however, ring true for me today, as I have echoed them first to my children and now they filter down to my grandchildren. Christmas calls us to a spirit of love and generosity, and with that spirit we can all be Santa's helpers. But oh what I would give for ears young enough to hear reindeer on my roof once more.

# Festive Christmas Dinners

"Tradition: sit with husband in a
room lit only by tree lights and
remember that our blessings
outnumber the lights."

- Betsy Cañas Garmon

# OVEN BBQ CRANBERRY CHICKEN
## (Quick, easy and delicious)

3-4 pounds chicken pieces or breasts
1/3 cup canola oil
1/3 cup onion, chopped
1/3 cup celery, chopped
1 ½ cups whole cranberry sauce
½ cup barbecue sauce

Brown chicken pieces in oil. Place chicken in a single layer in a ungreased baking dish. Sauté onion and celery until tender. Add cranberry sauce and barbecue sauce; stir until combined. Pour over chicken. Bake uncovered at 350° F. for 1 hour. Serves 4.

# CRANBERRY CHICKEN
## (Easy and festive!)

1 cup red onion, sliced
8-10 chicken breasts
1 cup cranberry sauce
1 tablespoon chicken bouillon

1 teaspoon vinegar
1 teaspoon mustard
1 ½ teaspoons salt

Place onion in slow cooker. Arrange chicken over onion. Combine remaining ingredients and spoon over chicken. Cover and cook on low for 6-8 hours or high 3-4 hours. Chicken can also be baked in oven at 350° F. for 1 ½ hours. Serve with rice.

# PIMENTO CHEESE-STUFFED CHICKEN BREASTS

4 chicken breasts, boneless and skinless
salt and pepper to taste
¾ cup cream cheese, softened
3 tablespoons pimentos, finely chopped
1 large clove garlic, grated or finely chopped
3 teaspoons paprika, divided
1 cup fine breadcrumbs
2 tablespoons canola oil

Preheat oven to 350° F. Butterfly chicken breasts so that they open up like a book. Place between layers of plastic wrap and pound to ¼ inch thickness. Season with salt and pepper. Combine cream cheese with pimentos, garlic and 1 teaspoon paprika; set aside. Combine remaining 2 teaspoons paprika with breadcrumbs in a flat dish. Spread a quarter of cream cheese mixture on each piece of chicken. Roll chicken pieces up and secure them with two toothpicks, then roll each piece in breadcrumbs. Heat oil in an oven safe skillet over medium-high heat. Brown chicken for a few minutes on each side, then transfer to oven and bake for 15-18 minutes, or until the juices run clear.

"My life has a superb cast but
I can't figure out the plot."
- Ashleigh Brilliant

# SPICY CHICKEN SPAGHETTI
## (A "welcome home" dish.)

1 -500 gram package of spaghetti
¼ cup butter
½ large onion, chopped
1 -450 gram box Velveeta cheese, cubed
1 can diced tomatoes and chilies
1 can cream of chicken soup
4 boneless chicken breasts, cooked and chopped

Cook spaghetti according to package directions, drain. Place spaghetti in a 9 x 13 inch greased baking dish. Melt butter in a large skillet over medium heat; add onion, and sauté 3-5 minutes or until tender. Add cheese and tomatoes, stirring until cheese melts. Stir in soup and chicken, blending well. Pour mixture over spaghetti. Bake at 350° F. for about 30 minutes or until bubbly. Makes 6 servings.


**I hate sex in the movies. Tried it once.
The seat folded up, the drink spilled and that ice,
well, it really chilled the mood.**

# EASY CHICKEN MANICOTTI
(This freezes very well, cook one pan and freeze the other.)

1 ½ pounds chicken breasts (4-5 breasts)
1 tablespoon garlic powder
16 uncooked manicotti shells
5 cups spaghetti sauce (divided)
1 pound Italian sausage, cooked and drained
250 grams (½ pound) mushrooms, sliced
4 cups mozzarella cheese, shredded
2/3 cup water

Rub garlic on raw chicken. Cut into 1 inch strips and stuff into shells. Spread 1 cup sauce in each of 2 greased 9 x 13 inch pans. Place 8 chicken stuffed shells in each pan. Sprinkle with sausage (crumbled or thinly sliced) and mushrooms. Pour remaining sauce over top. Sprinkle with cheese. Drizzle 1/3 cup water around edge of each dish. Cover with foil and bake in 350° F. oven for 65-70 minutes. Cover and freeze the other casserole. Thaw in fridge and bake. One pan serves 4 people.

*"If you see ten troubles coming down the road,
you can be sure that nine will run
into the ditch before they reach you."*
*- Calvin Coolidge*

# TURKEY PASTA BAKE
(Use whatever noodles or pasta you have on hand.)

250 grams pasta
1 can cream of chicken soup
2/3 cup milk
1 ½ cups Velveeta cheese, shredded
½ cup green pepper, chopped
¾ cup celery, chopped
2 ½ - 3 cups leftover chicken or turkey
½ cup flaked almonds

Cook and drain pasta. Place in bottom of greased casserole dish. Mix soup and milk and warm in microwave. Add cheese and stir until melted. Combine pepper, celery and turkey with soup mixture and pour over noodles. Sprinkle with almonds. Bake uncovered at 350° F. for 30 minutes.

*"Often people attempt to live their lives backwards;*
*they try to have more things, or more money,*
*in order to do more of what they want, so they will be*
*happier. The way it actually works is the reverse.*
*You must first be who you really are, then do*
*what you need to do, in order to have what you want."*
*- Margaret Young*

# TURKEY VEGETABLE CASSEROLE
## (Great way to use leftover turkey and vegetables.)

4 cups cooked vegetables (carrots/green beans/broccoli/
cauliflower)
2 cups cooked turkey, cubed
1 can cream of mushroom soup
½ cup milk
1 -250 gram package cream cheese
½ teaspoon dill weed
salt and pepper to taste
1 package turkey stove top stuffing

Put vegetables and turkey into a greased casserole dish. Mix
soup, milk, cream cheese, dill, salt and pepper. Pour over
vegetables and turkey. Stir to blend. Prepare stuffing according
to package directions, and spoon over turkey mixture.
Bake at 350° F. for about 1 hour, or until bubbling.

*"All the adversity I've had in my life, all my troubles
and obstacles, have strengthened me....You may not
realize it when it happens, but a kick in the teeth
may be the best thing in the world for you."*
*- Walt Disney*

# TURKEY SALAD TORTILLAS
## (December 27th — still leftover turkey!)

2 cups cooked turkey, cubed
1 cup Cheddar cheese, shredded
¾ cup celery, finely chopped
¼ cup onion, finely chopped
¼ cup ripe olives, sliced
½ cup mayonnaise
¼ cup salsa
¼ teaspoon salt
6 small flour tortillas

In a bowl combine turkey, cheese, celery, onion, olives, mayonnaise, salsa and salt. Spoon about ½ cup filling off centre on each tortilla. Fold sides and ends over filling, roll up. Place in a shallow microwave safe dish. Cover and microwave on high for 2-3 minutes or until cheese is melted and filling is hot, or bake for 15 minutes at 325° F.

"My idea of Christmas, whether old-fashioned or modern, is very simple: loving others. Come to think of it, why do we have to wait for Christmas to do that?"
- Bob Hope

# TURKEY LASAGNE
## (Surprise! More leftover turkey.)

3 cups fresh mushrooms, sliced

2 cups onion, chopped

2 tablespoons butter

2 packages Knorr Hollandaise sauce, prepared

6-8 lasagne noodles, cooked

2 pounds leftover turkey, thinly sliced

salt and pepper to taste

1 teaspoon dried basil

1 teaspoon dried oregano

3 cups mozzarella cheese, grated

1 cup Parmesan cheese, grated

2 -364 gram cans asparagus tips

Preheat oven to 350° F. Sauté mushrooms and onions in butter until soft. Spread a small amount of Hollandaise sauce on bottom of 9 x 13 inch pan. Place half of the following: noodles, turkey, salt and pepper to taste, mushrooms and onion mixture, Hollandaise sauce, basil and oregano, mozzarella cheese and Parmesan cheese. Place all asparagus in neat layers over cheese and then repeat all layers ending with cheese. Bake for 35-40 minutes. Let stand for 10 minutes before cutting and serving.

*Encouragement is oxygen for the soul.*

# TURKEY POT PIE
### (Leftover turkey can become a feast!)

4-5 cups turkey, cubed
1 ½ - 2 cups gravy
3 large carrots, sliced and partially cooked
2-3 large potatoes, cubed and partially cooked
1 ½ cups frozen peas
1 cup onions, chopped and sautéed
1 cup celery, chopped and sautéed
1 can cream of mushroom soup
½ - 1 cup water (depending on amount of leftover gravy)
salt and pepper to taste

2 deep dish double pie crusts

Mix all ingredients together. Put half of mixture in each crust and top with crusts. Bake at 400° F. for 10-15 minutes, and then reduce to 375° F. for 40 minutes.
It is lovely served with a salad and buns.

*"Three things in human life are important.*
*The first is to be kind. The second is to be kind.*
*And the third is to be kind."*
*- Henry James*

# TURKEY SCALLOPINI

1/3 cup flour
¼ teaspoon dried rosemary, crushed
¼ teaspoon dried thyme
1/8 teaspoon pepper
1 pound turkey cutlets
4 teaspoons canola oil
¼ cup white wine (or chicken broth)
½ teaspoon cornstarch
1/3 cup chicken broth
½ cup sour cream
1 teaspoon brown mustard
paprika to garnish

In a large plastic bag combine flour and spices. Add turkey and shake to coat. In a large non-stick skillet, cook turkey in oil over medium heat for 2-4 minutes on each side or until juices run clear. Remove and keep warm. Add wine to skillet; cook and stir for 30 seconds, stirring to loosen any brown bits from the pan. Combine cornstarch and broth until smooth, pour into skillet. Add sour cream and mustard and heat through. Bring to a boil; cook and stir for 2 minutes or until slightly thickened. Pour over turkey, sprinkle with paprika if desired. Great served with rice, pasta or a salad.

# THE CHRISTMAS TURKEY

(Since the turkey is the centre of the Christmas Dinner
let us share some of the points we have learned after
cooking more than 300 Christmas dinners!)

- Roast turkey in a large, sturdy, shallow roasting pan so that the entire turkey will cook all the way through.

- Buy 1 to 1 ½ pounds of turkey a person – this will allow for some leftovers.

- Allow 24 hours of thawing time in the fridge for every 4 pounds of turkey. Thawed turkeys keep for 2 days in the fridge. If your turkey is still too icy on Christmas morning and it is time to get going – place the bird in a sink full of cold water; change the water every 30 minutes. Do not use warm water.

- Stuffing: allow ¾ cup per pound of turkey. Stuff turkey just before roasting. Loosely spoon stuffing into neck and body cavities; pull skin over stuffing and secure to turkey with short skewer or sew opening shut with kitchen string.

- After stuffing, tuck drumsticks under the band of skin across tail, or tie legs to tail with kitchen string.

- Place turkey, breast side up, on rack of roasting pan. Brush with butter or cooking oil. Cover loosely with foil, or cover with lid. Place in preheated 375° F. oven. Once you hear the turkey begin to sizzle and cook, turn oven down to 325° F. After two-thirds of cooking time, cut string between drumsticks. Remove the foil or lid for the last 30-45 minutes of cooking.

Continued on next page.................

# THE CHRISTMAS TURKEY continued.........

- Use the following chart for roasting times- (unstuffed turkeys of the same weight take 45 minutes less to cook through. The centre of the dressing inside the bird must reach a temperature of 165° F. for food safety. For an unstuffed turkey, place the meat thermometer in the thickest part of the thigh, taking care that it does not touch any bone. Roast the turkey until the meat thermometer reaches 180 °F.

| Approximate Roasting Times for Stuffed Turkey | | Unstuffed Turkey |
|---|---|---|
| Turkey Weight | Roast Time | Roast Time |
| 6 to 8 pounds | 3 to 3 ½ hours | 2 ½ to 3 hours |
| 8 to 12 pounds | 3 ½ to 4 ½ | 3 to 4 hours |
| 12 to 16 pounds | 4 ½ to 5 ½ | 4 to 5 hours |
| 16 to 20 pounds | 5 ½ to 6 hours | 5 to 5 ½ hours |
| 20 to 24 pounds | 6 to 6 ½ | 5 ½ to 6 hours |

- To serve turkey; remove stuffing to a serving bowl and cover with foil to keep warm. Allow turkey to stand covered with foil for 15-20 minutes to allow meat to firm up. Then use a sharp knife and slice lightly to avoid shredding the meat. Remove drumsticks and thighs. Then carve off breast meat in one piece. Place breast portion on the platter and carve into slices. Finally remove wings. Carve thigh meat from the bones. If none of your guests want an entire drumstick to themselves, carve meat from drumsticks as well. When putting the platter together, be creative; grapes or small oranges and fresh herb sprigs add a decorative touch to the platter.

# TURKEY PAN GRAVY
## (In place of the drippings ¼ cup melted butter can be used in this recipe.)

pan drippings from roasted turkey
¼ cup flour
1 ¾ cups chicken broth
salt and black pepper

After roasting, transfer turkey to cutting board. Pour pan drippings into a 2 cup measuring cup. Scrape browned bits from pan into cup. Skim and reserve ¼ cup fat from drippings, discard the rest. Pour ¼ cup fat into a medium saucepan. Stir in flour. Add enough broth to remaining drippings in measuring cup to equal 2 cups. Add broth mixture all at once to flour mixture in saucepan. Cook and stir over medium heat until thickened and bubbly. Cook and stir 1 minute more. Season to taste with salt and pepper. Makes 2 cups.

- Refrigerate meat, stuffing and gravy separately. Eat or freeze within two days.

"Christmas – that magic blanket that wraps itself about us, that something so intangible, that it is like a fragrance.
It may weave a spell of nostalgia."
- Augusta E. Rundell

# TURKEY STUFFING/DRESSING
(This recipe will stuff a 12-14 pound turkey.)

1 ½ cups butter or margarine
2 medium onions, chopped
4 sticks celery, chopped
2 medium carrots, chopped
8-10 cups stale bread, cubed
water
7 eggs, beaten
½ teaspoon salt
½ teaspoon pepper
3 teaspoons poultry seasoning

Sauté onions, celery and carrots in butter. Place cubed bread in a large bowl, sprinkle some water over all. Bread should be moist not soggy. Add eggs, salt, pepper, poultry seasoning and sautéed mixture to bread. Mix well. At this point, mixture should feel moist. If mixture is too dry add an extra egg or ¼ cup of melted butter. Additional salt, pepper, and poultry seasoning may be added to taste. Be sure your turkey cavity is dry prior to stuffing. When turkey is cooked, remove dressing from cavity. Arrange neatly on plate with sliced turkey.

"To perceive Christmas through its wrapping
becomes more difficult with every year."
- E.B. White

Shown on previous page:

Molded Christmas Pudding — Page 155
Mashed Potato Layer Bake — Page 122
Sweet Corn Muffins — Page 56
Glazed Ham — Page 92
Red/Green Festive Salad — Page 109
Mustard Sauce — Page 136
Spiced Cranberry Orange Mold — Page 112
Classic Tortiére — Page 91

# BACON COLBY LASAGNE

1 pound ground beef
1 medium onion, chopped
1 pound bacon, cooked and crumbled
1 tablespoon sugar
½ teaspoon salt
1 -443 ml can tomato sauce
1 -414 ml can diced tomatoes
4-6 cups Colby cheese, shredded
9 lasagne noodles

Brown beef and onion; drain. Add bacon, sugar, salt, sauce
and tomatoes. Heat through. Meanwhile, cook noodles. Layer
in a greased 9 x 13 inch baking dish: 1 cup of sauce, cover with
3 noodles, next add 2 cups of sauce, then 1/3 of the Colby
cheese, 3 noodles, sauce, cheese and repeat layers one more
time. Bake at 350° F. for 45 minutes.

"Christmas is forever, not for just one day, for loving,
sharing, giving, are not to be put away like bells and
lights and tinsel, in some box upon a shelf.
The good you do for others is good you do yourself."
- Norman Wesley Brooks

# MEXICAN MEATLOAF

1 tablespoon canola oil
1 onion, diced
1 green pepper, diced
1 clove garlic, minced
1 tablespoon chili powder
salt and pepper to taste
1 egg
1 ½ pounds ground beef
1 cup kidney beans, drained and rinsed
½ cup bread crumbs
½ cup salsa
½ cup Cheddar cheese, shredded

In a large skillet, heat oil over medium heat. Add onion, green pepper and garlic. Cook until softened, about 5 minutes. Stir in chili powder, salt and pepper. In a large bowl, beat egg; mix in ground beef, kidney beans, bread crumbs and salsa. Mix in onion mixture to just combine. Pack into 4 x 8 inch greased loaf pan. Sprinkle with cheese. Bake at 350° F. for 60-70 minutes. Let stand 5 minutes before serving.

A conclusion is simply the place where you
land when you get tired of thinking.

# DOUBLE MEATSAUCE

4 tablespoons oil
3 onions, chopped
5-6 cloves garlic, crushed
1 pound ground beef
1 pound ground pork

Fry together until meat is thoroughly cooked.

## Add:

1 -156 ml can tomato paste
1 -1.36 litre of tomato juice
2 cans tomato soup
¼ teaspoon ground cinnamon
¼ teaspoon chili powder
¼ teaspoon ground cloves
4-5 bay leaves
salt and pepper to taste
1 teaspoon oregano
2 tablespoons white vinegar
2 tablespoons Worcestershire sauce
2 tablespoons brown sugar
½ cup ketchup
1 cup mushrooms, chopped

Simmer until well blended. Serve over pasta of your choice.

# SLOW COOKER BEEF STEW

3 pounds beef stew meat

2 tablespoons flour

½ teaspoon salt

3 tablespoons canola oil

1 cup baby carrots

4 large potatoes, cubed

1 tablespoon dried parsley

1 teaspoon pepper

2 cups boiling water

1 package dry onion soup mix

3 tablespoons butter

1 medium onion, sliced

¼ cup red wine

¼ cup flour

¼ cup warm water

Place meat in a large plastic bag, add 2 tablespoons flour and salt and shake to coat. Heat oil in large skillet over medium-high heat, add stew meat and cook until evenly browned. Transfer to slow cooker and add carrots, potatoes, parsley and pepper. In a small bowl stir together water and soup mix, pour into slow cooker. In the same skillet melt butter and sauté onions until softened, remove to slow cooker. Pour red wine into skillet and stir to loosen browned bits of food on the bottom, pour into slow cooker. Cover and cook on high for 30 minutes, reduce heat to low and cook 6 hours or until meat is fork tender. In a small bowl or cup mix together ¼ cup flour and warm water, stir into stew and cook uncovered for 15 minutes or until thickened.

*Hope is a wonderful thing – one little nibble will keep a man fishing all day.*

# TATER TOT CASSEROLE

1 ½ pounds lean hamburger
2 cups frozen peas
1 medium onion, thinly sliced
1 bag tater tots
1 can mushroom soup
1 can Cheddar cheese soup
½ cup of water

Put raw hamburger in the bottom of greased 9 x 13 inch baking dish. Cover with layer of frozen peas, layer of onions, and tater tots. Mix soups and water; pour over casserole.
Bake at 350° F. for 1 ½ hours.
Hint: Prepare just before you bake.

"Every time a hand reaches out to
help another....that is Christmas.
Every time someone puts anger aside and
strives for understanding ...that is Christmas.
Every time people forget their differences and realize
their love for each other....that is Christmas.
May this Christmas bring us closer to the
spirit of human understanding.
Closer to the blessing of peace!"
- Author Unknown

# RUEBEN BAKED POTATOES
## (A meal in itself!)

4 large baking potatoes
2 cups corned beef
1 cup sauerkraut, drained, chopped
1 cup Swiss cheese, shredded
3 tablespoons green onions, chopped
1 garlic clove, minced
¼ cup prepared horseradish sauce
1 teaspoon caraway seed
1 -250 gram package cream cheese, softened
¼ cup Parmesan cheese, grated
¼ teaspoon paprika

Preheat oven to 425° F. Bake potatoes until tender and let cool. Cut potatoes in half and scoop out flesh, leaving skins intact. Save skins and potato. Dice corned beef and place in bowl. Add sauerkraut and Swiss cheese, green onions, garlic, horseradish sauce and caraway seed. In another bowl mash potatoes with cream cheese and stir into corned beef mixture. Mound filling in potato skins and top with Parmesan and sprinkle with paprika. Bake for 30-40 minutes and serve immediately.

*"Embrace the detours."*
*- Kevin Charbeneau*

# BACON WRAPPED PORK TENDERLOIN

1 pound bacon, lightly browned but not crisp, drained
1 tablespoon garlic powder
1 teaspoon seasoning salt
1 teaspoon basil
1 teaspoon oregano
2 small pork tenderloins, cut into 1 ½ inch medallions
2 tablespoons butter or margarine
2 tablespoons canola oil

Combine garlic, salt, basil, and oregano. Set aside. Wrap bacon around tenderloin and secure with toothpick. Heat butter and oil in skillet. Dip meat into spices and brown 4 minutes on each side. Bake 17-20 minutes at 400° F. or until meat is no longer pink.

# OVEN RIBS

4 pounds pork spareribs
¼ cup ketchup
¼ cup Worcestershire sauce
½ cup chili sauce
1 teaspoon dry mustard

1 cup brown sugar
¼ cup soy sauce
¼ cup rum
2 cloves garlic, crushed
dash ground black pepper

Preheat oven to 350° F. Cut spareribs into serving size portions, place ribs in a large roasting pan. In a bowl, mix together the rest of ingredients. Coat ribs with sauce and bake for 2 hours; baste after one hour.

# GLAZED PORK TENDERLOIN
(This is a great meal to have during the holiday
season; a nice change from turkey and ham.)

2 pounds pork tenderloin
¼ cup butter, softened
salt and pepper to taste
1 teaspoon ground thyme
2 teaspoons garlic powder
2 cups apricot preserves
2 tablespoons honey, or to taste
¼ cup white wine or apple juice

Preheat oven to 350° F. Spread butter over pork tenderloin.
Season with salt, pepper, and thyme. Combine garlic powder,
apricot preserves, honey, and wine or juice in a separate bowl.
Roast pork in oven for 30-40 minutes. Remove pork from oven
and brush with apricot mixture. Return pork to oven. Continue
roasting, basting occasionally with remaining sauce, until pork is
no longer pink in centre, about 15 minutes or until an internal
temperature of 160° F.

*"A year spent making mistakes is not only
more honourable, but more useful than
a year spent doing nothing."*
*- G.B. Shaw*

# CLASSIC TOURTIÈRE

1 ½ cups potato, peeled and cubed
1 pound lean ground pork
1 pound lean ground beef
2 cups mushrooms, sliced
¾ cup chicken stock
¾ cup celery, finely chopped
2 onions, finely chopped
3 cloves garlic, minced
¾ teaspoon salt
½ teaspoon each: pepper, dried savory and thyme
¼ teaspoon each: ground cloves and ground cinnamon
1 bay leaf
1 egg yolk

1 double large (or two double small) deep dish pie shells

In a covered saucepan of boiling salted water, cook potato until
tender, about 10 minutes. Drain, mash and set aside.
In deep skillet, sauté pork and beef over medium high heat,
mashing with fork until no longer pink. Drain off fat and
add rest of ingredients, except egg yolk and potatoes. Bring to a
boil. Reduce heat, cover, simmer, until almost no liquid remains,
about 25 minutes. Discard bay leaf. Mix in potatoes. Let cool.
Place mixture into pie shell, brush pie rim with water, top with
pastry, seal, trim and flute. Brush top of pie with egg yolk mixed
with 1 tablespoon water. Bake in bottom third of 400° F. oven
for 50 minutes until golden.

# GLAZED HAM

6 pounds ready to serve ham, bone in, rind on
whole cloves
pineapple chunks
maraschino cherries, halved
½ cup brown sugar
1 teaspoon mustard powder
3 tablespoons frozen orange juice

With sharp knife, score rind in triangle pattern about ¼ inch deep. Place ham in roaster. Cover. Bake in 350° F. oven for 2 hours. Remove from oven and cut rind off ham. Increase oven heat to 450° F. Push a whole clove into each triangle. Secure pineapple and cherry halves with toothpicks; place here and there over ham. Mix sugar, mustard powder and orange juice to a paste. Brush over surface of ham. Bake uncovered about 15 minutes to glaze. Spoon drippings over ham at half time. Internal temperature should read 140° F. when done. Serves 8.

Note: Ham that is labelled "Fully Cooked" or "Ready to Eat", may be eaten cold, as is, with no further preparation; but it will taste and look better if heated thoroughly, to an internal temperature of 140° F. and glazed during the latter part of cooking. Allow 18-20 minutes of cooking per pound.
Ham labelled "Cook before Eating" needs roasting to an internal temperature of 160° F. Allow 20 minutes of cooking per pound.

# APRICOT GLAZED SALMON

6 teaspoons honey
1 teaspoon lemon zest, grated
juice of 2 lemons
¼ cup Marsala wine (or another sweet wine)
¼ cup apricot jam
4 -6 ounce salmon portions, skinless, boneless
salt and pepper

Preheat oven broiler.  Combine honey, lemon zest, juice of lemons, wine, and jam in a saucepan.  Cook, stirring constantly over medium heat until sauce thickens, about 5 minutes. Place salmon on a greased broiler pan and season with salt and pepper. Broil about 4 or 5 inches from the heating element for approximately 10-12 minutes or until salmon flakes apart. Spoon half the apricot mixture over salmon the last 3 minutes of cooking.  Serve remaining sauce with salmon.

"It is Christmas every time you let God love others through you...yes, it is Christmas every time you smile at your brother and offer him your hand."
                                        - Mother Teresa

# POTATO CRUSTED SALMON
# WITH PICKLE SAUCE

2 Russet potatoes, baked and chilled
2 tablespoons horseradish
2 tablespoons oil
salt and pepper
4 -6 ounce salmon fillets

Preheat oven to 375° F. Grate potatoes through large holes of a box grater into a medium sized bowl. Stir in horseradish, oil, salt and pepper mixing well. Pat mixture onto top surface of fillets forming a crust and place in baking pan or on baking sheet. Bake until salmon is cooked through and the crust is golden and crispy, about 15 minutes. Serve with Pickle Sauce.

Pickle Sauce:
2 dill pickles, chopped
1 small bunch dill, chopped
1 green onion, chopped
1 tablespoon mustard
½ cup mayonnaise
juice from half a lemon
salt and pepper

Put all ingredients for pickle sauce in a bowl and mix well.

# PECAN CRUSTED TILAPIA

4 -6 ounce tilapia fillets
½ cup dry breadcrumbs
2 tablespoons pecans, finely chopped
½ teaspoon salt
¼ teaspoon garlic powder
¼ teaspoon black pepper
½ cup buttermilk
½ teaspoon hot sauce (like Tabasco)
3 tablespoons flour
1 tablespoon canola oil, divided
lemon wedges

Combine breadcrumbs, pecans, salt, garlic, and pepper in a
shallow dish. Combine buttermilk and hot sauce in a medium
bowl. Place flour in a third dish. Dredge 1 fillet in flour, dip into
buttermilk mixture, then into breadcrumb mixture. Repeat with
remaining fillets. Heat 1 ½ teaspoons oil in a large skillet (non-
stick works best) over medium-high heat. Cook 2 fillets for 3
minutes on each side or until fish flakes easily. Add remaining oil
and cook additional 2 fillets. Serve with lemon!

*Sometimes one little spark of kindness is all
it takes to reignite the lights of hope in a
heart that's blinded by pain.*

# SHRIMP SCAMPI

(This is a great main course recipe, but may also be
used as an appetizer, serving smaller portions.)

1 ½ pounds large shrimp (about 16 to 24)

1/3 cup clarified butter*

4 tablespoons garlic, minced

6 green onions, thinly sliced

¼ cup dry white wine

2 tablespoons lemon juice, fresh if possible

2 tablespoons fresh parsley, chopped

salt and pepper, to taste

2 Roma tomatoes, diced

Rinse shrimp and set aside. Heat butter in large skillet over medium
heat. Cook garlic 1-2 minutes or until softened but not browned.
Add shrimp, green onions, wine and lemon juice; cook until shrimp
are pink and firm, about 1-2 minutes on each side. Do not overcook.
Add parsley, salt and pepper before serving. Toss in the tomatoes
and garnish with lemon slices and parsley sprigs if desired. Serve
with angel hair pasta and a green salad for a favourite restaurant
quality meal.

*Clarified butter is butter that has had the milk solids and water
removed. One advantage of clarified butter is that it has a much higher
smoke point, so you can cook with it at higher temperatures without it
browning and burning. Also, without the milk solids, clarified butter can
be kept for much longer without going rancid. It is very easy to make.
Melt the butter slowly. Let it sit for a bit to separate. Skim off the foam
that rises to the top, and gently pour the butter off of the milk solids,
which have settled to the bottom. A stick (8 tablespoons) of butter will
produce about 6 tablespoons of clarified butter.

# I'll Be Home For Christmas

I had been diagnosed with a rare and advanced form of small cell ovarian cancer in September, 1989. The doctors told me that I'd be lucky to see the new year. My stage four cancer was terminal they told me because of the large in-operable tumours wrapped around my aorta. They told me there was really nothing that they could do for me. I begged my healthcare team not to give up on me as I hadn't given up on myself. "Together we can make medical history" I pleaded with them. My family and friends believed in me, and that gave me the strength and determination to keep on living and facing cancer head on. After several months of gruelling cancer treatment, I was shocked to learn that I would have to be in the hospital for the holidays as extensive surgery was required at precisely the right time following my chemotherapy session.

On Christmas Eve when my family and friends walked past the nursing station, they were told that they better call before coming in on Christmas morning. "We don't think she'll make it through the night" they said. But I did!

That was over twenty years ago. Today I am proud to be living a very active and fulfilling life. As Executive Director for the Canadian Cosmetic, Toiletry and Fragrance Association Foundation, through our work with Look Good Feel Better, I am both grateful and blessed to be able give back and support other lives affected by cancer.

The song "I'll be home for Christmas" truly resonates with me and I am grateful that the gift of health is the greatest gift of all.

Merry Christmas to all!

**SHERRY ABBOTT**
EXECUTIVE DIRECTOR,
Canadian Cosmetic, Toiletry and Fragrance Assn. Fnd.

# WARNING......WARNING...... CHRISTMAS VIRUS

Be on the alert for symptoms of inner **Hope, Peace, Joy and Love**. The hearts of a great many have already been exposed to this virus and it is possible that people everywhere could come down with it in epidemic proportions. This could pose a serious threat to what has, up to now, been a fairly stable condition of conflict in the world.

Some signs and symptoms of **The Christmas Virus:**

A tendency to think and act spontaneously rather than on fears based on past experiences.

An unmistakable ability to enjoy each moment.

A loss of interest in judging other people.

A loss of interest in interpreting the actions of others.

A loss of interest in conflict.

A loss of the ability to worry. (This is a very serious symptom.)

Frequent, overwhelming episodes of appreciation.

Contented feelings of connectedness with others and nature.

Frequent attacks of smiling.

An increasing tendency to let things happen rather than make them happen.

An increased susceptibility to the love extended by others as well as the uncontrollable urge to extend it.

# Seasonal Side Dishes and Salads

"Never worry about the size of your
Christmas tree. In the eyes of
children, they are all ten feet tall."

- Larry Wilde

# ALMOND ORANGE SALAD

1 head leaf lettuce or Romaine lettuce, torn
2 green onions, finely chopped
2 mandarin oranges or 1 -284 ml can mandarins, drained
1 ripe avocado, peeled and sliced
½ cup sunflower seeds
½ cup sliced almonds
2 tablespoons butter

Dressing:
½ cup canola oil
3 tablespoons red wine vinegar
1 tablespoon lemon juice
2 teaspoons sugar
½ teaspoon salt
½ teaspoon dry mustard
1 garlic clove, crushed

Mix lettuce, onions, mandarins and avocado in a large salad bowl. Sauté sunflower seeds and almonds in butter. Cool and add to salad. Mix dressing ingredients together. Toss salad with dressing just before serving.

**I read recipes the same way I read science fiction,**
**- I get to the end and think,**
**Well, that's not gonna happen.**

# APPLE AND BLUE CHEESE SLAW

3-4 red apples, sliced
1 cup green cabbage, shredded
1 cup red cabbage, shredded
1 cup blue cheese salad dressing
1 tablespoon sweet onion, grated
1 tablespoon red wine vinegar
¼ cup blue cheese, crumbled

Combine apples and cabbage in medium bowl. Mix salad dressing, onion and vinegar in another bowl. Pour half of dressing over salad, stir to mix and add blue cheese. Add more dressing as desired. Serve chilled.

# APPLE SALAD

1 -4 serving size package instant butterscotch pudding
1 ½ cups milk
1 cup whipped topping
3 cups apples, chopped
1 cup crushed pineapple in juice
½ cup grapes
1 cup miniature marshmallows
½ cup walnuts, optional

Mix pudding with milk until thick, add whipped topping. Mix apples, pineapple, grapes, and marshmallows. Stir fruit into pudding mixture. Cool at least 1 hour before serving. Garnish with walnuts. Makes 12 servings.

# BALSAMIC CRANBERRY SALAD

mixed greens
½ cup pecans, toasted
1/3 cup red onion, thinly sliced
1/3 cup dried cranberries
4 tablespoons Feta cheese, crumbled

Dressing:
1/3 cup olive oil
2 tablespoons balsamic vinegar
¼ teaspoon salt
1/8 teaspoon pepper
1 tablespoon sugar

Mix greens, nuts, onion, cranberries, and cheese in large bowl. In a measuring cup, mix dressing ingredients in order given and blend well. Pour over greens just before serving.


"The Act of God designation on all insurance policies....means roughly that you cannot be insured for the accidents that are most likely to happen to you. If your ox kicks a hole in your neighbour's Maserati, however, indemnity is instantaneous."
- Alan Coren

# CHRISTMAS SALAD
## (Delicious and attractive!)

½ cup pecan halves
1 -120 gram package mixed spring greens
½ cup dried sweetened cranberries
½ cup red onion, thinly sliced
¼ cup canola oil
2 tablespoons soy sauce
2 ½ tablespoons balsamic vinegar
2 tablespoons brown sugar
1 teaspoon ginger
½ teaspoon dried red pepper flakes
½ cup blue cheese or goat cheese, crumbled

Lightly brown pecans in skillet for 2-3 minutes. Cool.
Place greens, cranberries and onion in salad bowl. Shake
together until well blended: oil, soy sauce, vinegar, sugar, ginger
and pepper flakes. Pour dressing over lettuce mixture; toss
gently, yet thoroughly to coat evenly. Top with pecans and
cheese. Serve immediately.
Makes 4 servings.

"Don't expect too much of Christmas Day. You can't crowd
into it any arrears of unselfishness and kindliness that may
have accrued during the past twelve months."
- Oren Arnold

# CHRISTMAS CRANBERRY MOLD

(Pretty pink with red flecks, tasty alternative to cranberry sauce.)

2 -7 gram packages of unflavoured gelatin

1 cup water

1 -398 ml can whole cranberry sauce

1 -398 ml can pineapple, drained

1 cup low fat plain yogurt or light sour cream

1/3 cup icing sugar

Sprinkle gelatin over ½ cup of the water in small saucepan. Let stand one minute. Heat and stir until dissolved. Add rest of water. Pour into medium bowl. Stir in remaining ingredients. Chill, stirring and scraping down sides often, until it shows signs of thickening. Pour into six cup mold. Chill.

"There are many in this old world of ours who hold that things break about even for all of us. I have observed for example that we all get the same amount of ice. The rich get it in the summertime and the poor get it in the winter."
- Bat Masterson

# CHRISTMAS VEGETABLE SALAD

¼ cup canola oil
1 tablespoon plus 1 ½ teaspoons lemon juice
1 tablespoon plus 1 ½ teaspoons white wine vinegar
1 teaspoon salt
½ teaspoon sugar
coarsely ground pepper
2 cups cauliflower, thinly sliced
½ cup pimiento-stuffed olives, sliced
1/3 cup green pepper, chopped
1/3 cup red pepper, chopped

In a jar with a tight-fitting lid, combine the first six ingredients; shake well. In a salad bowl, combine the cauliflower, olives and peppers; drizzle with dressing and toss to coat. Cover and refrigerate for several hours or overnight. Yield: 6-8 servings.

*"The amount of satisfaction you get from life depends largely on your own ingenuity, self-sufficiency, and resourcefulness. People who wait around for life to supply their satisfaction usually find boredom instead."*
*-Dr. William Menninger*

# CREAMY APPLE SALAD

1 cup whipping/heavy cream

¼ cup icing sugar

½ teaspoon vanilla

6-8 apples, peeled and cut into bite size pieces

½ cup 7up or Sprite

Whip cream until almost thick. Add icing sugar and vanilla and whip until set. Coat apple pieces with pop to keep from browning. Drain apples and add to whipped cream mixture. Refrigerate and serve as soon as possible.

# CREAMY CRANBERRY APPLE SALAD

3 cups cranberries, fresh or frozen, thawed and coarsely chopped

2 ½ cups unsweetened crushed pineapple, drained

2 cups miniature marshmallows

1 medium apple, chopped

2/3 cup sugar

1/8 teaspoon salt

2 cups whipping/heavy cream

¼ cup walnuts, chopped

In a large bowl, combine the cranberries, pineapple, marshmallows, apple, sugar and salt. Cover and refrigerate overnight. Just before serving, beat cream until stiff peaks form. Fold cream and walnuts into the cranberry mixture. Yield: 14 servings.

# FRUIT SALAD

(Great way to enjoy your fruit, brunch or dessert.
Add any fruit you wish and it will be delicious.)

4 cups strawberries, sliced
3 cups seedless green grapes
½ cantaloupe, peeled and chopped
2 -284 ml cans mandarin oranges with juice/or 3 fresh
mandarin oranges
2 -398 ml cans sliced peaches with juice
½ fresh pineapple, cubed (optional)
½ honey dew, cubed
4 kiwi, peeled and sliced
sugar/sweetener to taste  (optional)

Mix all fruit together.
Serve with whipped cream or with ice cream for dessert.


*"Love the animals, love the plants; love everything. If you
love everything you will perceive the divine mystery in
things. Once you perceive it, you will begin to comprehend
it better every day, and you will come at last to love the
whole world with an all embracing love."*
*- Fyodor Dostoyevsky*

# LENTIL SALAD

1 -473 ml can of lentils, drained and rinsed
1 large carrot, diced
2 large celery stalks, diced
1 red pepper, diced
½ red onion or 2 green onions, diced

Dressing:
¼ cup olive oil
¼ cup red wine vinegar
2 tablespoons Dijon mustard
½ teaspoon salt
1 teaspoon dried oregano
¼ teaspoon pepper
¼ - ½ (to taste) cup fresh Parmesan cheese, grated

Combine all vegetables in a large bowl. Combine dressing
ingredients.  Add to vegetables and lentils, mix.
Add Parmesan and toss.

* Note: other vegetables can be substituted or added, kee p the
chopped size consistent with the other veggies. Dried
cranberries also go well with this salad.

# MEDITERRANEAN QUINOA SALAD

2 cups water
2 cubes chicken bouillon
1 clove garlic
1 cup uncooked quinoa
2 large chicken breasts, cooked and cut into bite size pieces
1 large red onion, diced
1 large green pepper, diced
½ cup black olives, chopped
½ cup feta cheese, crumbled
¼ cup fresh parsley, chopped
¼ cup fresh chives, chopped
½ teaspoon salt
1/3 cup fresh lemon juice
1 tablespoon balsamic vinegar
¼ cup olive oil

Bring water, bouillon cubes, and garlic to a boil in a saucepan. Stir in quinoa, reduce heat to medium-low, cover, and simmer until quinoa is tender and the water has been absorbed, 15-20 minutes. Discard garlic clove and scrape quinoa into a large bowl. Gently stir chicken, onion, pepper, olives, cheese, parsley, chives, and salt into quinoa. Drizzle with lemon juice, balsamic vinegar, and oil. Stir until evenly mixed. Serve warm or refrigerate and serve cold.

# POMEGRANATE SALAD
(Looks especially festive at Christmas time.)

1 -140 gram bag spring salad mix
½ red and green peppers, sliced thin
raspberry vinaigrette dressing
1 pomegranate, seeded
½ cup almonds (optional)

Toss salad mix with peppers. Add dressing. Top with pomegranate and almonds.


# RED/GREEN FESTIVE SALAD
(Attractive, delicious addition to any yuletide table.)

4 cups mixed salad greens, torn
2 tablespoons green onion, sliced
2 medium red apples, diced
2 kiwi fruit, peeled and sliced
1 cup raspberries, unsweetened
½ cup poppy seed salad dressing

Toss the salad greens, onion and fruit in a bowl. Drizzle with dressing. Serve immediately.

# ROMAINE SALAD WITH
# SWEET CRANBERRY DRESSING

¾ cup pecans, toasted
½ teaspoon seasoning salt
3 hearts of Romaine lettuce
1 cup Craisins (dried cranberries)
½ cup red onion, finely chopped

Dressing:
1/3 cup vinegar
¾ cup canola oil
¼ cup sugar
¼ cup whole cranberry sauce
¼ cup Miracle Whip
¼ teaspoon salt
1/8 teaspoon pepper

Sprinkle seasoning salt on pecans, and toast pecans in oven or a skillet until lightly browned – watch closely as this doesn't take long; cool. Prepare lettuce salad, tossing Craisins, onion and pecans together in a large bowl. Whisk all dressing ingredients together and refrigerate until just before serving time. Toss dressing with salad and serve.

"Never do anything that you wouldn't
want to explain to the paramedics."
- Author Unknown

# SALAD CUPS

12 slices bread, white or whole wheat
3 tablespoons butter, melted
1 ½ cups lettuce, chopped
¼ cup carrots, chopped
¼ cup grape tomatoes, chopped
favourite salad dressing

Preheat oven to 400° F. Use a rolling pin to slightly roll out each slice of bread. Cut out 2-3 inch rounds, insert in greased muffin tin pressing down slightly and forming cup shape. Lightly brush each one with melted butter. Bake for 8-10 minutes until lightly brown and crispy. Cool. Remove bread cups from tins and fill with lettuce, carrots and tomatoes tossed with dressing.
Note: Use Caesar salad sprinkled with Parmesan cheese.

# SAUERKRAUT SALAD

1 -796 ml can sauerkraut
2 cups celery, chopped
1 green pepper, chopped
2 green onions, chopped
Bring above ingredients to a boil and cool to lukewarm.
Add:
1 ½ cups sugar
¼ cup canola oil
½ cup vinegar
Mix all ingredients well. Refrigerate at least 2 hours before serving.

# SPICED CRANBERRY ORANGE MOLD
## (Wonderful salad for Christmas dinner.)

2 -4 serving size packages cranberry jelly powder
1 ½ cups boiling water
1 -398 ml can whole cranberry sauce
¾ cup cold water
1 tablespoon lemon juice
¼ teaspoon ground cinnamon
1 orange, sectioned and diced

Dissolve jelly in boiling water. Stir in cranberry sauce. Stir in cold water, lemon juice and cinnamon. Chill about 1 ½ hours or until mixture starts to thicken. Stir in orange. Spoon into a 5 cup mould. Chill until firm, about 4 hours. Turn out onto plate by dipping mould in hot water for about 10 seconds and gently pulling jelly from around the edges with moist fingers.
Makes 8 servings.

**Often the difference between a successful marriage and a mediocre one consists of leaving about three or four things a day unsaid.**

# SPINACH WITH FRUIT SALAD

4 cups spinach, washed and torn
1 cup strawberries, sliced
½ cup green grapes, halved
½ cup red grapes, halved
¼ cup sunflower seeds, toasted

Mix all together and toss with Poppy Seed Dressing

Poppy Seed Dressing:
2 tablespoons peanut oil
2 tablespoons balsamic vinegar
1 tablespoon maple syrup
1 tablespoon poppy seeds
¼ teaspoon salt

Mix all together and pour over spinach salad.
Yield: 6-8 servings.

"Christmas begins about the first of December with an office
party and ends when you finally realize what you spent,
around April fifteenth of the next year."
- P.J. O'Rourke

# SPINACH SALAD
## (A colourful, tangy salad.)

2/3 cup canola oil
1/4 cup red wine vinegar
2 teaspoons lemon juice
2 teaspoons soy sauce
1 teaspoon sugar
1 teaspoon dry mustard
1/2 teaspoon curry powder
1/2 teaspoon salt
1/2 teaspoon pepper
1/4 teaspoon garlic powder
4-6 cups fresh spinach, torn
5 bacon strips, cooked and crumbled
2 hard-boiled eggs, sliced

In a small bowl, whisk the first 10 ingredients; set aside. Place spinach in a large salad bowl. Just before serving, whisk dressing again and drizzle over spinach; toss gently. Garnish with bacon and egg slices. Yield: 6-8 servings.

"The earth has grown old with its burden of care,
But at Christmas it always is young."
- Phillips Brooks

# GINGERED ORANGE BEETS

1 ½ pounds whole fresh beets (about 4 medium), trimmed and cleaned
6 tablespoons olive oil, divided
¼ teaspoon salt
¼ teaspoon white pepper
1 tablespoon rice vinegar
1 tablespoon orange juice concentrate
1 ½ teaspoons orange zest, grated
½ teaspoon fresh gingerroot, minced
1 medium navel orange, peeled, sectioned and chopped
1/3 cup pecan halves, toasted

Preheat oven to 425° F.  Brush beets with 4 tablespoons oil; sprinkle with salt and pepper.  Wrap loosely in foil; place on baking sheet.  Bake for 70-75 minutes or until fork-tender. Cool slightly.  In a small bowl, whisk vinegar, orange juice, 1 teaspoon orange zest, ginger and remaining oil; set aside. Peel beets and cut into wedges; place in a serving bowl.  Add the orange sections and pecans.  Drizzle with orange sauce and toss to coat.  Sprinkle with remaining orange zest.


"It's frustrating when you know all the answers, but
nobody bothers to ask you the questions."
- Author Unknown


115

# CARROT AND HORSERADISH CASSEROLE

8 - 10 large whole carrots, cooked in salted water until tender
1 small onion, sliced in long strips
¼ cup carrot liquid
½ cup mayonnaise
1 tablespoon creamed horseradish
salt and pepper
¼ cup cracker crumbs, finely crushed
2 tablespoons butter, melted
sprinkle of parsley
sprinkle of paprika

Arrange onions on the bottom of a 9 x 13 inch greased casserole dish. Slice cooked carrots into thin strips and place them over onions. Mix carrot liquid, mayonnaise, horseradish and salt and pepper and pour over vegetables. Blend butter and crumbs and sprinkle over carrot mixture. Sprinkle with parsley and paprika. Bake 25 minutes at 350° F.

"The trouble with, 'A place for everything and everything in its place' is that there's always more everything than places."
- Robert Brault

# CRAN-ORANGE GLAZED CARROTS
## (This is a celebration style carrot... very tasty.)

5 cups carrots, cut into about ½ inch slices
½ cup butter, softened, cubed
½ cup jellied cranberry sauce
orange peel strip (2-5 inches)
4 tablespoons brown sugar
¾ teaspoon salt

Place a little water in a skillet, bring carrots to a boil. Reduce heat; cover and simmer for about 15 minutes or until tender crisp.
Meanwhile, in a blender, combine butter, cranberry sauce, orange peel, brown sugar and salt. Cover and process until blended. Drain carrots, drizzle with cranberry mixture.
Serves about 8 people.

Christmas is a time when kids tell Santa what they want and adults pay for it. Deficits are when adults tell the government what they want and their kids pay for it.

# WHIPPED CARROTS WITH CRANBERRIES

4 - 5 large carrots, sliced
3 tablespoons butter
1 tablespoon brown sugar
½ teaspoon ground ginger
¼ teaspoon salt
¼ cup dried cranberries

Place carrots in saucepan with water. Bring to a boil. Reduce heat; cover and simmer for 15-20 minutes or until tender. Drain. Place carrots in a food processor; add butter, brown sugar, ginger and salt. Cover and process until smooth. Transfer to a serving bowl, stir in cranberries. Yield: 4 servings.


# MARINATED PORTOBELLO MUSHROOM

1 large Portobello mushroom
1 teaspoon soy sauce
1 teaspoon balsamic vinegar
1 teaspoon canola oil
¼ teaspoon sugar
sprinkle of garlic powder

Place mushroom with cap side down in a shallow baking dish. Mix remaining ingredients and sprinkle over mushroom. Marinate for several hours. Bake 15 minutes at 400° F. Slice and serve.

# DECKED OUT PEAS
(Deck the peas with basil and mustard ... tasty variation)

Dressing:
¼ cup water
1 teaspoon cornstarch
2 tablespoons red wine vinegar
1 teaspoon sugar
1 teaspoon sweet basil
1 teaspoon prepared mustard
¼ teaspoon salt
pinch of pepper
pinch of ground nutmeg
1 kg bag frozen peas

Measure all ingredients except peas in a saucepan. Heat and stir until mixture comes to a boil and thickens slightly. Cook peas. Drain. Add dressing to warm peas just before serving. Stir. Serves 10-12.

"Show me a woman who doesn't feel guilt and I'll show you a man."
- Erica Jong

# SQUASH-APPLE BAKE

1 medium buttercup or butternut squash, peeled and cut into
¾ inch slices
2 medium apples, peeled and cut into wedges
½ cup brown sugar, packed
1 tablespoon flour
¼ cup butter, melted
½ teaspoon salt
½ teaspoon ground mace

Preheat oven to 350° F. Arrange squash in medium greased baking dish. Top with apple wedges. Combine remaining ingredients; spoon over apples. Bake uncovered, 50-60 minutes or until tender. Yield: 4-6 servings.

# CANDIED SWEET POTATOES

1 large or 2 medium sweet potatoes or yams
½ cup pecan pieces
¾ cup brown sugar
½ cup margarine or butter, melted

Boil potato in water until tender. When cooked remove from water and place in fridge overnight. After cooled peel potato, cut in half lengthwise and then cut into 4 again. Lay with flat side on a baking dish sprayed with Pam. Place pecan pieces on each piece of potato. Combine sugar and butter until creamy. Pour over potatoes and bake uncovered 30 minutes at 350° F.

# ROASTED WINTER ROOT VEGETABLES

1 onion, cut into chunks
3 carrots, cut into 1 inch pieces
1 large sweet potato, cut into 1 inch cubes
3 parsnips, cubed
2 turnips, cut into 1 inch cubes
¼ cup olive oil
salt, pepper and basil or thyme to taste
* beets and white potatoes can also be used in this dish

Preheat oven to 400° F. Place onion, carrots, sweet potato, parsnips, and turnips into a large mixing bowl. Drizzle with olive oil, and toss to coat. Season to taste with spices, and place vegetables into a shallow roasting pan so they are not layered too deep. Roast until vegetables have lightly browned around edges and are tender, about 45 minutes. Stir once as vegetables roast to ensure even cooking.

*"Anger and rage only detour you from your final objectives. The future holds nothing but opportunity, and good things happen to good people. I promise."*
*- Matt Hardy*

# MASHED POTATO LAYER BAKE
## (The first dish gone at the pot-luck, and everyone wanted the recipe!!)

4 large white potatoes, peeled and cooked
2 large sweet potatoes or yams, peeled and cooked
1 -250 gram tub chive and onion cream cheese, divided
½ cup sour cream, divided
¼ teaspoon salt
¼ teaspoon pepper
¼ cup Parmesan cheese, grated, divided
¼ cup Cheddar cheese, shredded, divided

Preheat oven to 375° F. Place white and sweet potatoes
in separate bowls. Add half of sour cream and cream cheese to
potatoes in each bowl, season with salt and pepper.
Mash until creamy. Stir half of Parmesan cheese into white
potatoes, and half of Cheddar cheese into sweet potatoes.
Alternately layer potatoes and sweet potatoes into a medium clear
casserole dish. Bake 15 minutes. Sprinkle with remaining cheeses
and bake 5 more minutes or until cheese is melted. Makes 14
servings - ½ cup each.

**Lead me not into temptation. I can find it myself.**

# ROASTED RED POTATOES
# WITH BACON & CHEESE
(Tastes like the hot potato salad at a favourite restaurant.)

½ cup ranch dressing
½ cup cheese, shredded (Italiano 4 cheese or cheese of choice)
¼ cup bacon, crumbled or real bacon bits
1 kg small red potatoes, quartered
2 tablespoons green onion, chopped (fresh parsley works well)

Preheat oven to 350° F. Mix dressing, cheese and bacon bits in large bowl. Add potatoes and toss until coated. Spoon into a lightly greased 9 x 13 inch baking dish. Cover with foil and bake for 40 minutes. Remove foil and bake an additional 15 minutes or until potatoes are tender. Garnish with green onion.

*"Don't say you don't have enough time. You have exactly the same number of hours per day that were given to Helen Keller, Pasteur, Michelangelo, Mother Teresa, Leonardo da Vinci, Thomas Jefferson, and Albert Einstein."*
*- H. Jackson Brown*

# PEROSHKI
## (Baked Perogy....a Ukrainian dish)

1 cup warm water
1 teaspoon sugar
1 tablespoon yeast
1 cup milk
2 tablespoons sugar
¼ cup butter or margarine
¼ cup canola oil
2 eggs
1 teaspoon salt
5 cups flour

Preheat oven to 350° F.
Mix first 3 ingredients and let rise for 10 minutes. Scald milk and cool. Add the cooled milk, and yeast mixture to the remaining ingredients. Mix and let rise 1 hour. Roll out dough in small batches and cut out circles with a soup can. Fill with potato filling and fold over. Place pinched end down on greased cookie sheet. Bake for approximately 20 minutes or until golden brown.

Continued on next page.............

# PEROSHKI

continued......

Potato Filling:
9 medium potatoes
2 cups cottage cheese
2 tablespoons dill
2 tablespoons green onion (optional)

Cook and mash potatoes. Add cheese, dill and onion. Mix together well.

Cream Sauce with Dill:
2 green onions, chopped
2 tablespoons butter
1 tablespoon flour
1 cup whipping/heavy cream
dill, fresh or dried

Fry onions in butter for 2 minutes. Add flour, stir and cook for 1 minute. Add cream and bring to a boil until sauce thickens. Add dill as desired. Serve over peroshki.

*"Enjoy the little things in life, for one day you may look back and realize they were the big things."*
*- Antonio Smith*

# LAZY MAN'S PEROGIES

8-10 lasagne noodles
10 medium potatoes, cooked and mashed
2-3 cloves garlic, minced
dollop of butter
½ - 1 cup cream
salt and pepper to taste
2 onions, chopped
½ cup margarine
2 cups Cheddar cheese, grated

Preheat oven to 350° F. Prepare lasagne noodles according to package directions. Oven ready lasagne noodles will work fine also. Prepare mashed potatoes by adding garlic, butter, cream, salt and pepper. Fry onions in margarine until cooked.
Layer 9 x 13 inch casserole with ½ of the following: mashed potato mixture, fried onions, Cheddar, lasagne noodles.
Repeat. Cover casserole with foil and bake for 45 minutes. Serve with sour cream.

"Oh look, yet another Christmas TV special! How touching
to have the meaning of Christmas brought to us by cola,
fast food, and beer....Who'd have ever guessed
that product consumption, popular entertainment,
and spirituality would mix so harmoniously?"
- Bill Watterson

# CURRY RICE WITH CHEDDAR
## (A great side dish or a quick and nourishing meal in itself!)

3 cups basmati rice, cooked
1 cup cherry tomatoes, halved
1 cup seeded cucumber, diced
1 cup yellow bell pepper, diced
1 cup green grapes, halved
¼ cup red onion, chopped
1 teaspoon curry powder
¼ cup olive oil
3 tablespoons white wine vinegar
2/3 cup aged Cheddar cheese, diced
salt and pepper to taste

Toss rice with fruit and vegetables. In a small bowl, combine curry, oil and vinegar, and drizzle over rice mixture. Toss to coat. Add cheese, salt and pepper, toss and serve.
Suggestion: You can add raisins, apples, nuts or whatever you prefer. Cheese variations also work great!

"The Christmas season has come to mean the period when the public plays Santa Claus to the merchants."
- John Andrew Holmes

# SASKATCHEWAN COUSCOUS

1 ¾ cups of chicken broth
½ cup cold water
¼ teaspoon white pepper
1 cup couscous
1 cup seedless green grapes, quartered
2 tablespoons fresh mint, chopped
1/3 cup pine nuts
1 teaspoon chives, minced (optional)
fresh mint sprigs for garnish

Place broth, water and pepper in saucepan and bring to a boil.
Add couscous and reduce heat and simmer until tender. Stir
frequently. Remove from heat, and stir in grapes, mint, pine
nuts and chives. Garnish with mint leaves.

It is easy to think Christmas, and it is easy to believe
Christmas, but it is hard to act Christmas.

# SLOW COOKER STUFFING

1 cup onion, diced
1 cup celery, diced
½ cup margarine or butter, melted
10 - 11 cups day-old bread, cubed
1 teaspoon salt
¼ teaspoon pepper
2 teaspoons poultry seasoning (or more to taste)
1 tablespoon parsley flakes (optional)
2 cups chicken or turkey broth

Sauté onions and celery in melted butter until tender. Place bread cubes and seasonings in large bowl. Pour butter mixture over cubes of bread and then add broth while stirring lightly to moisten all bread. Bread should be moist but not soggy. Pack lightly into slow cooker. Cover and set on high for one hour, and turn to low and cook 1 hour more, or you may cook on low for 5 to 6 hours. Stir lightly as needed.
*Add cooking time if you lift the lid of the slow cooker while cooking — heat decreases each time.
*Your turkey will roast more quickly without stuffing in the cavity. Sprinkle poultry seasoning in cavity, add an onion and roast.

# LAZY CABBAGE ROLLS

Cabbage rolls are delicious and add so much to a Christmas dinner, but also take a lot of time and work in preparation. Lazy cabbage rolls are a good substitution — you get the same flavour with less preparation time. Our group had three different kinds in their recipe boxes, so we are sharing all three.

## BUCKWHEAT CABBAGE ROLLS

(Buckwheat has a distinct taste but those who grew up with it will crave these at Christmas time.)

2 cups whole buckwheat
4 cups water
1 teaspoon salt
1 medium onion, finely chopped
½ cup butter
4 cups cabbage, shredded
dash pepper
¼ cup butter
½ cup onion, finely chopped

Bring buckwheat and salted water to a boil. Cover tightly and simmer for 20 minutes. Preheat oven to 325° F.
Sauté onion and cabbage with butter, add pepper. Mix buckwheat with onion and cabbage and place in greased casserole dish. In a small fry pan sauté onion and butter. Spread over casserole mixture and bake covered for 40 minutes.

130

# LAZY CABBAGE ROLLS
(You can use packaged coleslaw to speed up the preparation, and make these a "really" lazy cabbage roll recipe!)

1 tablespoon canola oil
1 pound lean ground beef
1 ½ cups onions, chopped
2 cloves garlic, finely chopped
1 -398 ml can tomato sauce
1 ¾ cups water
½ cup long grain rice
1 teaspoon chicken or beef bouillon mix
½ teaspoon salt
¼ teaspoon freshly ground pepper
1/8 teaspoon ground nutmeg
6 cups cabbage, shredded
sour cream

Heat oil in large frying pan over medium heat. Add beef, onions and garlic. Cook, stirring to break up beef, until browned. Drain off excess fat. Stir in tomato sauce, water, rice, bouillon, salt, pepper, and nutmeg. Bring to a boil. Reduce heat and simmer, covered, for 20-25 minutes or until rice is tender and liquid is thickened. Sprinkle half of cabbage over bottom of a greased 9 x 13 inch baking dish.

Continued on next page........

# LAZY CABBAGE ROLLS continued......

Spoon half of beef mixture over cabbage and spread evenly. Sprinkle remaining cabbage. Spread remaining beef mixture over top. Bake covered at 350° F. for 1 hour or until bubbly and heated through. Serve with sour cream.

Note: If desired, 2 -284 ml cans of tomato soup may be substituted for the tomato sauce. If using tomato soup, reduce water to 1 cup.

# GERMAN SOUR LAZY CABBAGE ROLLS

¾ cup long grain rice
2 cups water
½ teaspoon salt
12 slices bacon, fried crisp and crumbled
2 onions, chopped
1 -398 ml can sauerkraut, drained and rinsed
salt and pepper to taste

Preheat oven to 325° F. Cook rice in water and salt until almost done. Add bacon, onions, sauerkraut, salt and pepper to rice. Put into greased medium casserole. Bake covered for 45 minutes.

# LEMON DILL SAUCE
## (Great on any type of fish.)

½ cup butter
2 tablespoons flour
1 chicken bouillon cube
½ teaspoon dill
¼ teaspoon salt
1 cup chicken broth
3 tablespoons lemon juice
3 tablespoons cream

Melt butter, add flour, bouillon cube, dill, and salt, stirring well. Add broth, lemon juice, and cream. Cook on low heat, stirring continually, until thickened. Serve warm.

"Let me not wrap, stack, box, bag, tie, tag,
bundle, seal, keep Christmas.
Christmas kept is liable to mold.
Let me give Christmas away, unwrapped,
by exuberant armfuls.
Let me share, dance, live Christmas unpretentiously,
merrily, responsibly with overflowing hands,
tireless steps and sparkling eyes.
Christmas given away will stay fresh
even until it comes again."
- Let Me Not Keep Christmas......Linda Felver

# EASY SUMPTUOUS ALFREDO SAUCE

(A delicious simple sauce to serve with your favourite pasta.)

½ cup butter

2 tablespoons cream cheese

2 cups whipping/heavy cream

2 teaspoons garlic powder

1 tablespoon parsley, chopped or flakes

1 teaspoon salt

pepper to taste

½ cup Parmesan cheese, grated

Melt butter, add cream cheese and stir until melted. Add cream, season with garlic, parsley, salt and pepper. Simmer for 15 minutes; it will thicken as it simmers. Stir in Parmesan cheese.

*"The family. We were a strange little band of characters trudging through life sharing diseases and toothpaste, coveting one another's desserts, hiding shampoo, borrowing money, locking each other out of our rooms, inflicting pain and kissing to heal it in the same instant, loving, laughing, defending, and trying to figure out the common thread that bound us all together."*
*- Erma Bombeck*

# CRANBERRY CITRUS SAUCE
## (Unique flavour, delicious twist on this holiday condiment!)

1 ½ cups fresh or frozen cranberries
zest from ½ orange
1 cinnamon stick
1 cup orange juice
1 cup brown sugar
water

In a medium saucepan, combine cranberries, orange zest, cinnamon, orange juice and brown sugar. Add enough water to cover, bring to a boil over high heat. Immediately reduce heat and simmer for about one hour, or until the sauce has thickened. Remove cinnamon stick. Let mixture cool, then refrigerate in a closed container. Serves 10-12 people. This recipe is easily doubled.

"Christmas gift suggestions:
To your enemy, forgiveness.
To an opponent, tolerance.
To a friend, your heart.
To a customer, service.
To all, charity.
To every child, a good example.
To yourself, respect."
- Oren Arnold

# MUSTARD SAUCE
(This "oh-so-good" mustard sauce has
become a staple in our fridge.)

½ cup sugar
2 teaspoons dry mustard
2 eggs, well beaten
1/3 cup vinegar
1 tablespoon butter

Place sugar, dry mustard, eggs and vinegar in a 2 cup glass
measuring bowl. Whisk. Microwave on high for 2-3 minutes,
whisking several times after the first minute, until mixture comes to
a boil and is thickened. Stir often. Stir in butter and cool.
Keep refrigerated. Great with cold meats, sausage or fish.


# FRUIT GLAZE FOR HAM
(Makes a beautiful tangy delicious glaze.)

1 -398 ml can unsweetened crushed pineapple, drained
½ cup apricot jam
1 tablespoon spicy brown mustard
2 teaspoons prepared horseradish

Combine above ingredients and spread over ham about 45
minutes before it is done roasting.

# White Envelopes

*It's just a small, white envelope stuck among the branches of our Christmas tree. No name, no identification, no inscription. It has peeked through the branches of our tree for the past 10 years or so. It all began because my husband Mike hated Christmas---oh, not the true meaning of Christmas, but the commercial aspects of it- overspending...the frantic running around at the last minute to get a tie for Uncle Harry and the dusting powder for Grandma---the gifts given in desperation because you couldn't think of anything else. Knowing he felt this way, I decided one year to bypass the usual shirts, sweaters, ties and so forth. I reached for something special just for Mike. The inspiration came in an unusual way. Our son Kevin, who was 12 that year, was wrestling at the junior level at the school he attended; and shortly before Christmas, there was a non-league match against a team sponsored by an inner-city church, mostly black.*

*These youngsters, dressed in sneakers so ragged that shoestrings seemed to be the only thing holding them together, presented a sharp contrast to our boys in their spiffy blue and gold uniforms and sparkling new wrestling shoes.*

*As the match began, I was alarmed to see that the other team was wrestling without headgear, a kind of light helmet designed to protect a wrestler's ears.*

*It was a luxury the ragtag team obviously could not afford. Well, we ended up walloping them. We took every weight class. And as each of their boys got up from the mat, he swaggered around in his tatters with false bravado, a kind of street pride that couldn't acknowledge defeat. Mike, seated beside me, shook his head sadly, "I wish just one of them could have won," he said. "They have a lot of potential, but losing like this could take the heart right out of them. Mike loved kids-all kids-and he knew them, having coached little league football, baseball and lacrosse. That's when the idea for his present came. That afternoon, I went to a local sporting* goods store and bought an assortment of wrestling headgear and shoes and sent them anonymously to the inner-city church.

On Christmas Eve, I placed the envelope on the tree, the note inside telling Mike what I had done and that this was his gift from me. His smile was the brightest thing about Christmas that year and in succeeding years.

For each Christmas, I followed the tradition---one year sending a group of mentally handicapped youngsters to a hockey game, another year a check to a pair of elderly brothers whose home had burned to the ground the week before Christmas, and on and on. The envelope became the highlight of our Christmas. It was always the last thing opened on Christmas morning and our children, ignoring their new toys, would stand with wide-eyed anticipation as their dad lifted the envelope from the tree to reveal its contents. As the children grew, the toys gave way to more practical presents, but the envelope never lost its allure. The story doesn't end there. You see, we lost Mike last year due to dreaded cancer. When Christmas rolled around, I was still so wrapped in grief that I barely got the tree up. But Christmas Eve found me placing an envelope on the tree, and in the morning, it was joined by three more. Each of our children, unbeknownst to the others, had placed an envelope on the tree for their dad.

This story was written by Nancy W. Gavin and was first published in Woman's Day Magazine in 1982

# Joyous
# Christmas
# Desserts

*"Love is what's in the room with you
at Christmas if you stop opening
presents and listen."*

- Author unknown, attributed to child named Bobby

# CRANBERRY UPSIDE DOWN CAKE
## (Quick, easy and delicious, great for a Christmas pot-luck)

1 -540 ml can pineapple tidbits
water
½ cup butter, melted
⅔ cup brown sugar, packed
1 cup cranberries, fresh or frozen
½ cup pecan halves
1 package yellow cake mix
3 eggs
¼ cup canola oil

Drain pineapple, reserving juice. Add water to juice to measure 1 ¼ cups, set aside. Pour butter into a greased 9 x 13 inch baking dish. Sprinkle with brown sugar, cranberries and pecans. Top with pineapple. In a mixing bowl, combine dry cake mix, eggs, oil, and reserved pineapple juice. Beat on medium speed for two minutes. Pour over ingredients in pan. Bake at 350° F. for 40 minutes, or until a toothpick inserted near the centre comes out clean. Cool for 10 minutes before inverting onto a large serving platter. Great with a dollop of whipped cream. Serves 12-16.

Why is Christmas just like a day at the office?
You do all the work and the fat guy with
the suit gets all the credit!

# CRANAPPLE STREUSEL PIE

4 cups apples, peeled and sliced
2 cups fresh cranberries
⅓ cup flour
1 cup sugar
1 teaspoon apple pie spice or ground cinnamon
single prepared unbaked pie shell

Streusel mixture:
⅓ cup flour
4 tablespoons butter or margarine
¼ cup sugar
½ teaspoon ground cinnamon

Mix apples, cranberries, flour, sugar and spice. Toss together and turn into pie shell. Mix together streusel mixture and spoon on top of fruit. Bake at 425° F. for 50-60 minutes.

I hate housework! You make the beds, do the dishes and six months later you have to do it all over again!!

# EASY CHRISTMAS ICE CREAM PIE

1 ½ cups chocolate wafers, finely crushed
5 tablespoons butter, melted
4 cups pistachio or mint chip ice cream
½ cup hot fudge sauce
small red and green candies

Mix wafer crumbs and butter, press into a pie plate, covering bottom and sides. Freeze for 30 minutes. Fill with softened ice cream, cover with fudge sauce and sprinkle with candies. Freeze before slicing and serving.


# COCONUT BREAD PUDDING
(This is an old family favourite, it will become your favourite too!)

3 slices of bread, cubed (white tastes best in this recipe)
2 cups milk
2 egg yolks, beaten
½ cup sugar
½ cup sweetened flaked coconut
1 teaspoon vanilla

Soak bread in milk in a greased casserole dish. Add egg yolks, sugar, coconut, and vanilla. Stir. Bake for 30 minutes at 350° F. Serves 4.

# FREEZER CARAMEL DRIZZLE PIE
## (Makes two delicious pies — and you will need two!)

2 prepared graham wafer pie crusts
6 tablespoons butter
1 cup shredded coconut
1 cup pecans, chopped
1 can sweetened condensed milk
1 -250 gram package cream cheese, softened
2 cups frozen whipped topping, thawed
1 ½ cups caramel ice cream topping

Place butter in a medium skillet and melt over medium heat. Add coconut and pecans, stirring to coat. Sauté until coconut and pecans are lightly toasted, about 5 minutes. Set aside. In a large mixing bowl, whip together condensed milk and cream cheese until fluffy. Fold in whipped topping. Spoon ¼ of cream cheese mixture into each graham cracker crust. Drizzle each with ¼ of caramel topping. Repeat layers with remaining cream cheese mixture and caramel. Top each pie with coconut and pecan mixture. Freeze overnight.

"There is a remarkable breakdown of taste and intelligence at Christmastime. Mature, responsible grown men wear neckties made of holly leaves and drink alcoholic beverages with raw egg yolks and cottage cheese in them."
- P.J. O'Rourke

# CHOCOLATE YULE LOG
(Easy jelly roll with cream cheese filling.
A chocolate lover's Christmas wish!)

1 -450 gram package white angel food cake mix
½ cup cocoa, sifted
icing sugar

Line cookie sheet with greased parchment paper. Prepare angel food mix according to package directions and add cocoa. Spread batter in prepared pan. Bake at 350° F. for about 15 minutes or until cake springs back when lightly touched. Cool in pan 10 minutes, then invert on to clean tea towel which has been sprinkled with icing sugar. Remove pan and paper and roll cake in tea towel. Cool rolled cake thoroughly.

Filling:
¾ cup chocolate chips
3 tablespoons hot brewed coffee
1 -250 gram package cream cheese
2 teaspoons vanilla
2 cups icing sugar

Combine chocolate chips and coffee in microwave safe bowl. Microwave and stir every 30 seconds until melted. Cool to room temperature.

Continued on next page .....

# CHOCOLATE YULE LOG continued.....

Beat cream cheese, vanilla, and icing sugar until just smooth. Add cooled chocolate mixture and stir to combine. Unroll cooled cake and spread with chocolate cream cheese filling. Re-roll and place on serving dish. Chill while preparing ganache.

Ganache:
¾ cup heavy/whipping cream
1 cup chocolate chips

In a medium sauce pan bring cream to a boil stirring constantly. Remove from heat and add chocolate chips. Mix until chips are melted. Cover pan and let sit 10 minutes. Remove cover and let cool until spreadable consistency is achieved. Spread over chilled cake and decorate with fork to resemble bark.

"Once again we find ourselves enmeshed in the Holiday Season, that very special time of year when we join with our loved ones in sharing centuries-old traditions such as trying to find a parking space at the mall. We traditionally do this in my family by driving around the parking lot until we see a shopper emerge from the mall, then we follow her, in very much the same spirit as the Three Wise Men, who thousands of years ago followed a star, week after week, until it led them to a parking space."   - Dave Barry

# CHRISTMAS PUDDING
(Traditional Christmas pudding like Grandma used to make!)

**Step 1**

Mix together:

1 ½ cups dry bread crumbs

1 cup seedless raisins

1 cup candied cherries and pineapple

½ cup currents

⅓ cup citron peel

¼ cup almonds, chopped

1 ½ cups flour

1 teaspoon baking powder

¾ teaspoon baking soda

1 ½ teaspoons salt

1 ½ teaspoons ground cinnamon

¼ teaspoon ground nutmeg

¼ teaspoon ground cloves

¼ teaspoon ginger

¼ teaspoon allspice

1 cup shortening

1 cup apples, grated

1 cup carrots, grated

1 cup potatoes, grated

**Step 2**

Mix together:

2 eggs

1 cup brown sugar

¼ cup liquid honey

Beat until fluffy.

Mix ingredients from Step 1 and Step 2 together.

Fill jars ¾ full. Steam 3 ½ hours in canner. Makes 7 pints.

Serve warm with brown sugar sauce or whipped cream sauce.

# BROWN SUGAR SAUCE

1 cup brown sugar, packed
¼ cup flour
½ teaspoon salt
2 cups water
1 teaspoon vanilla

Mix well; sugar, flour and salt in a medium saucepan. Stir in water and vanilla. Heat and stir over medium heat until it boils and thickens. Serve over Christmas Pudding.

# WHIPPED CREAM SAUCE

1 cup milk
½ cup flour
2 egg yolks
½ cup sugar
½ cup butter
2 egg whites
1 teaspoon vanilla
1 cup whipping/heavy cream, whipped

Mix milk, flour, egg yolks, sugar and butter in double boiler and cook until real thick. Cool. Beat egg whites and vanilla until stiff. Fold into milk mixture. Fold in whipped cream. First part may be made a day ahead, and whip cream added 2 hours before serving. Serve over Christmas Pudding.

# DEATH BY CHOCOLATE
(Especially for the chocolate lovers - it is to die for!)

1 chocolate cake mix
1 cup chocolate sauce
2 -4 serving packages of chocolate instant pudding, prepared
2 tubs whipped topping
1 cup Skor chips

Prepare cake mix according to directions, bake on a greased cookie sheet, cool. Cut into 2 cm squares. Put half of cake pieces in the bottom of a large clear bowl. Drizzle ½ cup of chocolate sauce on cake. Spread ½ of pudding over the top. Spread 1 tub of whipped topping on pudding and sprinkle with ½ cup of chips. Repeat layers. Chill. Scoop through all layers when serving. Serves many!

"Until one feels the spirit of Christmas, there is no Christmas. All else is outward display, so much tinsel and decorations. For it isn't the holly, it isn't the snow.
It isn't the tree, not the firelight's glow.
It's the warmth that comes to the hearts of men when the Christmas spirit returns again."
- Anonymous

147

# FESTIVE TRIFLE

1 ½ cups boiling water

2 -4 serving size packages of cherry jelly powder

1 ½ cups cold water

1 -540 ml can cherry pie filling

4 cups angel food cake cubes

3 cups cold milk

2 -4 serving size packages of vanilla instant pudding

1 tub whipped topping

Dissolve jelly in boiling water. Stir in cold water and pie filling. Refrigerate about 1 hour or until slightly thickened. Place cake cubes in a large clear bowl. Spoon jelly mixture over cake. Refrigerate about 45 minutes or until set but not firm. Mix milk and pudding together for 1 minute. Gently stir in 2 cups of whipped topping. Spoon over jelly mixture. Refrigerate for 2 hours or until set. Top with remaining whipped topping and garnish if desired.

Women are angels
And when someone breaks our wings
We simply continue to fly—on a broomstick
We're flexible like that!

# MINCEMEAT CHEESECAKE
## (An interesting combination - awesome!)

1 ½ cups graham wafer crumbs

⅓ cup brown sugar

⅓ cup margarine, melted

Combine and press on bottom of a 9 inch ungreased spring form pan. Bake at 325° F. for 10 minutes.

2 -250 gram packages cream cheese

⅔ cup sugar

2 tablespoons flour

2 tablespoons lemon juice

1 tablespoon lemon rind, grated

½ teaspoon vanilla

2 eggs

2 cups mincemeat

Cream all ingredients together except the mincemeat. Pour mixture over the base. Spoon mincemeat over top and marble lightly by drawing spoon through mixture. Bake at 350° F. for 40-45 minutes. Cool completely before removing sides of pan. Chill before serving.

**When in charge, ponder**
**When in doubt, mumble**
**When in trouble, delegate.**

# MINCEMEAT MALLOW CAKE

1 cup vanilla wafer crumbs
¼ cup butter, melted
1 ¾ cups mincemeat
4 cups miniature marshmallows
⅓ cup orange juice
2 -250 gram packages cream cheese
2 teaspoons orange rind, grated
1 cup whipping cream, whipped
½ cup candied fruit or cherries

Combine crumbs with butter. Press on the bottom of a 9 inch ungreased spring form pan. Chill. Spread mincemeat over base. Melt marshmallows with orange juice. Stir until smooth; chill until slightly thickened. Combine cream cheese and orange rind. Beat until fluffy. Whip in marshmallow mixture, then fold in whipped cream. Pour over mincemeat layer and chill until firm. Garnish as a wreath with candied fruit and/or cherries.

"I love the Christmas-tide, and yet,
I notice this, each year I live;
I always like the gifts I get,
But how I love the gifts I give!"
- Carolyn Wells

# PISTACHIO DESSERT
## (Light and refreshing!)

1 cup flour
½ cup butter or margarine
¾ cup pecans, finely chopped
1 -250 gram package cream cheese
1 cup icing sugar
2 -4 serving size packages pistachio instant pudding mix
3 cups milk
1 ½ cups whipping/heavy cream
¾ cup icing sugar
1 ½ teaspoons vanilla

Mix flour and butter until crumbly. Stir in pecans, reserving ¼ cup for the top. Press crumbs into ungreased 9 x 13 inch pan. Bake at 350° F. for 15 minutes. Cool.
Mix cream cheese and 1 cup icing sugar together until smooth. Spread over the crust. Beat pudding mix with milk. Spread over the cheese layer and chill for 10 minutes until firm. Whip cream, add ¾ cup icing sugar, and vanilla. Spread over pudding layer and sprinkle with remaining pecans.

"There's nothing sadder in this world than to awake Christmas morning and not be a child."
- Erma Bombeck

# SUPREME CHERRY DESSERT

2 cups graham crumbs
½ cup butter, melted
4 tablespoons sugar
2 cups whipping/heavy cream, whipped
3 cups miniature marshmallows
4 tablespoons sugar
1 -540 ml can cherry pie filling

Mix crumbs, butter and 4 tablespoons sugar. Press into an ungreased 9 x 13 inch cake pan; reserve ¼ cup of crumbs for the top. Mix whipped cream, 4 tablespoons sugar, and marshmallows. Spread half of the mixture on crumbs. Spread pie filling over marshmallow mixture. Spread remaining marshmallow mixture over pie filling. Sprinkle with remaining crumbs. Chill several hours before serving. Serves 15.

*"People are like stained glass windows: they sparkle and shine when the sun is out, but when the darkness sets in, their true beauty is revealed only if there is light from within."*
*- E.K. Ross*

# TOBLERONE CARAMEL CHEESECAKE
## (Sweet and yummy!)

1 ¼ cups Oreo baking crumbs
¼ cup butter, melted
3 -250 gram packages cream cheese
¾ cup brown sugar
1 tablespoon vanilla
3 eggs
⅓ cup caramel ice cream topping
1 -100 gram bar Toblerone Swiss milk chocolate, coarsely chopped

Mix crumbs and butter, press in to an ungreased 9 inch spring form pan. Beat cream cheese, sugar, and vanilla until smooth. Add eggs 1 at a time, while continuing to mix. Pour over base. Bake at 350° F. for 40-45 minutes. Spread caramel topping over cheesecake just before serving, garnish with chocolate.


**Women are like phones. We love to be held, talked to, but if you press the wrong button you'll be disconnected.**

# DRIED FRUIT COMPOTE
(A traditional dish for families celebrating
Christmas by the Julian calendar.)

1 -375 gram package dried mixed fruit
¾ cup golden raisins
8 dried figs (optional)
¼ cup sugar (or to taste)
1 strip lemon rind (about an inch wide)
2 whole cloves
¼ teaspoon allspice

Place dried fruit in large pot. Pour in enough water to cover the fruit to about 2 inches above fruit. Bring to a slow boil over medium heat and simmer covered for about 15 minutes; stirring occasionally. Add sugar, lemon rind, cloves and allspice. Stir and add a little more water if necessary. Simmer gently uncovered for 10-15 minutes until fruit has softened. Remove lemon rind and cloves. Chill for several hours before serving.

"Christmas is for children. But it is for grown-ups too.
Even if it is a headache, a chore, and nightmare,
it is a period of necessary defrosting of
chill and hide-bound hearts."
- Lenora Mattingly Weber

# MOLDED CHRISTMAS PUDDING

(A "secret recipe" shared by a generous friend. A truly festive Christmas dessert that requires patience in the making.)

½ cup butter, softened

¾ cup brown sugar, packed

2 eggs

1 cup flour

1 cup fine, stale bread crumbs (not dry)

1 teaspoon baking soda

½ teaspoon salt

½ teaspoon ground cinnamon

½ teaspoon ground nutmeg

¼ teaspoon ground cloves

¼ teaspoon ground ginger

1 cup mixed fruit  (fruit cake mix)

1 cup dark raisins

½ cup golden raisins

¾ cup red cherries, halved (or red and green)

½ cup slivered almonds

⅓ cup dark rum

In a large bowl, cream butter with sugar until fluffy. Beat in eggs, one at a time. In a separate bowl, combine flour, bread crumbs, baking soda, and spices. Stir in fruit, raisins, cherries and almonds. With a wooden spoon, stir half of the dry

Continued on next page........

# MOLDED CHRISTMAS PUDDING

continued.....

ingredients into the creamed mixture. Add dark rum, then the remaining dry ingredients. Mix only until moistened. Line the bottom of a greased 8 cup pudding mold with a circle of greased waxed paper, pressing firmly into any patterns in the mold. Pack in the batter evenly. Cut another circle of waxed paper to fit over the batter, grease lightly and place on top. Cover with the mold lid and fasten in place. Place the mold on a wire rack in a large pot and pour in enough boiling water to come two-thirds up the side of the mold. Cover pot and simmer over medium-low heat, adding water as needed to maintain level for 2 ½ hours or until tester inserted in centre comes out clean. Let cool before removing the pudding from the mold. Overwrap and refrigerate for up to 4 weeks or freeze for up to 3 months. To reheat, return pudding to the mold and steam for 1 hour on the stove top. Or, microwave an individual serving. Serve with rum sauce or ice cream.

"The first fall of snow is not only an event, it is a magical event. You go to bed in one kind of world and wake up in another quite different, and if this is not enchantment then where is it to be found?"

- John B. Priestley

# CHRISTMAS FIGGY NUT PIE

1 prepared deep dish large pie crust

½ cup Calimyrna figs, chopped

3 tablespoons water

2 tablespoons orange marmalade

¾ cup brown sugar, packed

1 tablespoon cornstarch

3 eggs

1 cup corn syrup

6 tablespoons butter, melted

2 teaspoons vanilla

1 ½ cups deluxe mixed nuts

Topping:

1 cup heavy/whipping cream

2 tablespoons sugar

1 tablespoon orange marmalade

Line pie crust with heavy foil and bake at 450° F. for 8
minutes, remove foil and bake for a few minutes longer until
golden. Cool. In a small saucepan combine figs and water.
Cook and stir over low heat until water is absorbed. Remove
from heat and stir in marmalade. In a large bowl, whisk brown
sugar and cornstarch. Whisk in eggs, corn syrup, butter, vanilla
and fig mixture; stir in nuts. Pour into pastry shell. Bake at
300° F. for 1 ¼ hours or until set. Cover edges with foil
during the last 30 minutes to prevent over-browning. Cool.
In a small bowl, beat cream until thickened, add sugar and
marmalade; beat until stiff peaks form. Serve with pie.

# CRANBERRY PECAN PIE

prepared pie crust, unbaked
4 eggs
1 cup dark corn syrup
1 cup brown sugar
6 tablespoons butter, melted
1 teaspoon vanilla
1 ½ cups pecans, chopped
1 cup fresh cranberries, chopped
½ cup pecan halves
whipped cream for garnish

*Sugared Cranberries for garnish (optional) — see below

Preheat oven to 350° F. Whisk eggs, corn syrup, sugar, butter and vanilla. Stir in pecans and cranberries. Pour into pie crust. Top with pecan halves. Bake for 50 minutes or until almost set and centre jiggles slightly. Cool completely on rack. Garnish with whipped cream and sugared cranberries.
*Sugared Cranberries: Mix 1 teaspoon warm water with 1 teaspoon dried egg white until frothy. Using a fork, dip well-dried fresh cranberries, one at a time into mixture. Let excess drip off and transfer to a plate spread with sugar. Roll until coated. With dry fork, transfer cranberries to another plate to let dry.

# DECADENT AND FUN CHOCOLATE FONDUES

## CHOCOLATE CREAM FONDUE

8 squares semi-sweet chocolate

⅓ cup whipping/heavy cream

3 tablespoons brandy or Amaretto almond liqueur (optional)

Melt chocolate and whipping cream in microwave on medium for 2-3 minutes or in a saucepan on stove at medium low heat. Blend until smooth. Stir in brandy. (If you don't want to use liqueur, just use an extra 3 tablespoons of cream.) Transfer mixture to a fondue pot and keep warm.

## TOLL HOUSE CHOCOLATE FONDUE

2 cups semi-sweet chocolate chips

1 can sweetened condensed milk

1 cup milk

¼ cup butter

1 teaspoon vanilla

Combine chocolate chips, sweetened condensed milk, milk, butter and vanilla in a saucepan. Stir over medium low heat until chocolate is melted and mixture is smooth. Transfer the mixture to a fondue pot and keep warm to serve. Makes 3 cups.

Suggestions for dippers: strawberries, banana slices (thickly sliced) pineapple chunks, maraschino cherries, peeled wedges of kiwi fruit, pear or apple slices, cubes of cake, marshmallows, cookies, dried apricots. Nuts are good but tricky to dip with fondue forks.

# SPLURGE NO-BAKE OREO CHEESECAKE

Crust:

1 ¼ cups chocolate crumbs

3-4 tablespoons butter, melted

Combine crumbs and butter. Press into greased spring form cheesecake pan. Place in freezer while preparing filling.

Filling:

3 -250 gram packages cream cheese

1 cup sugar

1 ½ cups whipping/heavy cream, whipped until stiff peaks

24 Oreo cookies, chopped

Whip cream cheese until smooth. Add sugar and blend. Mix whipping cream and cream cheese together. Fold in the Oreo cookies. Pour filling onto crust and spread evenly. Cover and refrigerate at least 4 hours. Loosen cheesecake by running a knife around edges. Release sides of pan.

Frosting:

4 semi-sweet chocolate squares

½ cup whipping/heavy cream

½ teaspoon vanilla

Melt chocolate over low heat, stirring constantly. Cool slightly. Whisk in whipping cream and vanilla. Glaze top and sides of cheesecake with frosting. Place in refrigerator about 3 minutes until hard.

# STICKY PUDDING WITH TOFFEE SAUCE

1 ½ cups pitted dates, chopped
1 ½ cups water
½ cup butter
1 cup brown sugar

3 eggs
2 cups flour
1 teaspoon baking powder
½ teaspoon baking soda

Toffee Sauce:
1 cup whipping/heavy cream
1 cup brown sugar
½ cup butter

Preheat oven to 350° F. Combine dates and water in a medium-sized saucepan. Bring to a boil and simmer gently for 10 minutes, or until most of the liquid has been absorbed by the dates. Purée dates in a food processor or blender. With electric mixer, beat butter with brown sugar. Beat in eggs, one at a time. In a medium-sized bowl, mix flour with baking powder and baking soda. Add to the wet batter and then stir in puréed dates. Spoon batter into a buttered 9 x 13 inch baking dish, lined with parchment paper. Bake for 35-45 minutes or until the top feels firm when gently pressed in the centre. While pudding is cooking, make toffee sauce by combining cream, sugar and butter in a heavy-bottom saucepan. Bring to a boil, then simmer and stir constantly for about 3 minutes. Let cool slightly. When cake is done and cooled slightly, prick with a skewer to make lots of tiny holes. Spoon half of the toffee sauce over the cake. When ready to serve, top with remaining toffee sauce and whipped cream. Can be served warm or at room temperature. Serves 12.

# CHILLED CRANBERRY CHEESECAKE

1 ½ cups graham crumbs

2 tablespoons sugar

1 teaspoon orange zest, grated

⅓ cup margarine, melted

2 envelopes unflavoured gelatin

¼ cup orange juice

1 -250 gram package cream cheese, softened

1 teaspoon orange zest, grated

1 -398 ml can whole berry cranberry sauce

1 ½ cups whipping/heavy cream


Combine crumbs, sugar, 1 teaspoon zest and margarine. Press into greased 9 inch spring form pan. Bake 10 minutes at 350° F. Cool completely. In a small pan, sprinkle gelatin over orange juice and let stand 1 minute. Cook over low heat until gelatin is dissolved. Cool slightly. In a separate bowl beat cheese and orange zest. Beat in cranberry sauce and gelatin mixture until smooth. Beat whipping cream separately until stiff. Fold cheese and whipped cream mixtures together. Pour over crust.. Refrigerate 3-4 hours before serving. Run a knife around edge of pan and carefully remove sides of pan. Serve with a scoop of whipped cream.

# PUMPKIN PECAN PIE

¼ cup butter

1 ¼ cups ginger snap crumbs

1 ½ teaspoons vanilla

1 -398 ml can pumpkin

1 egg

1 egg white

½ cup brown sugar

½ teaspoon ground cinnamon

¼ teaspoon ground nutmeg

¼ teaspoon ground mace

½ cup brown sugar

4 tablespoons honey

4 tablespoons butter, melted

¾ cup pecans, chopped

Melt butter and mix with crumbs and vanilla. Press into pie plate. Bake 10 minutes at 350° F. Cool. Blend pumpkin, egg, egg white, ½ cup sugar and spices and spread over crust. Bake about 35-40 minutes or until an inserted knife comes out clean. Combine ½ cup sugar, honey, butter and pecans and pour over pumpkin mixture. Broil 2 minutes or until bubbly or golden brown.

What do you call people who are afraid of Santa Claus?
Claustrophic!

163

# CHOCOLATE SNOWBALL CAKE
## (For Easter, colour the coconut in pastel colours.)

1 -2 layer devil's food cake mix
1 -250 gram package cream cheese
1 egg
2 tablespoons sugar

In a 2.5 litre oven proof bowl, prepare cake according to directions on package. Blend cheese, egg and sugar; and spoon into centre of batter. Bake 60-70 minutes at 350° F. or until toothpick comes out clean. Cool.

Icing:
1 -4 serving package vanilla instant pudding
¼ cup icing sugar
1 cup milk
2 cups prepared whipped topping or whipped cream
1 cup flaked coconut

Beat pudding, icing sugar, and milk for 2 minutes. Fold in whipped topping mixture and refrigerate. Turn out cake onto plate and ice with pudding mixture. Sprinkle with coconut to give appearance of snow. Refrigerate until serving.

*"Life is like a hot bath. It feels good while you're in it, but the longer you stay in, the more wrinkled you get."*
*- Robert Oustin*

# PUMPKIN-SWIRL CHEESECAKE

2 cups ginger snaps, crushed
¼ cup pecans, finely chopped
¼ cup margarine, melted
3 -250 gram packages cream cheese
¾ cup sugar
1 teaspoon vanilla
3 eggs
1 cup pumpkin, mashed
1 teaspoon ground cinnamon
¼ teaspoon ground nutmeg
dash of ground cloves

Combine ginger snaps, pecans and margarine. Press into
9 inch greased spring form pan. Beat cheese, ½ cup sugar,
and vanilla until blended. Add eggs, beating well after each egg.
Remove 1 cup of batter. To remaining batter add: pumpkin,
spices and rest of sugar. Spoon ½ of pumpkin batter over
crumbs. Add plain batter, then remaining pumpkin batter.
Swirl with a knife. Bake 45 minutes at 350° F. or until centre
is almost set. Cool completely and refrigerate at least 4 hours
before serving. Serve with a bit of whipped cream on each slice.

Anyone who believes that men are equal to
women has never seen a man trying to
wrap a Christmas present.

# RHUBARB CHEESECAKE

1 cup flour

¼ cup sugar

½ cup butter or margarine

3 cups rhubarb, fresh or frozen*

½ cup sugar

3 tablespoons flour

2 -250 gram packages cream cheese

½ cup sugar

2 eggs

1 cup sour cream

2 tablespoons sugar

1 teaspoon vanilla


Blend flour, sugar and butter. Press into 9 inch greased spring form pan. In a separate bowl toss rhubarb, ½ cup sugar and flour. Mix cream cheese, ½ cup sugar and eggs until smooth and add rhubarb mixture. Pour over crust and bake at 350° F. for 40 minutes or until set. Mix sour cream, sugar and vanilla. Remove cake from oven and cover with sour cream mixture while still hot. Cool and refrigerate until serving.
* If you are using frozen rhubarb, bring rhubarb and ¼ cup water to a boil on the stove. Cook for 10 minutes, drain and let cool. Frozen rhubarb becomes a bit tough after it is frozen.

# LAZY CHEESECAKE
(Apple pie filling is the favourite at our house.)

2 -340 gram cans refrigerated crescent dinner rolls
2 -250 gram packages cream cheese, softened
1 cup sugar
1 tablespoon vanilla
1 -540 ml can pie filling (your choice)
½ cup butter, melted
Topping:
½ cup sugar
1 tablespoon ground cinnamon

Flatten one tube of crescent roll dough and press into bottom of a
greased 9 x 13 inch pan.  In a medium bowl, mix together:
cream cheese, 1 cup sugar, and vanilla until smooth.  Spread
cream cheese mixture over dough in pan.  Spread pie filling over
cream cheese mixture.  Unroll remaining crescent roll dough and
place over top of cream cheese layer.  Spread melted butter over
top and sprinkle with topping mixture.  Bake in 350° F. oven
for 30 minutes, or until top is lightly toasted.  Cool and
refrigerate before serving.

**My idea of a super bowl is a toilet that cleans itself.**

**Cancer and Christmas** – these words seem to be a contradiction, and yet for so many Christmas is spent colored by this disease.

Our daughter was almost a year, the precious gift of her first Christmas with us fast approaching. My parents had accepted an invitation to head south, joining their "snowbird" relatives, sharing their spacious motor home and the warm, sunny winter in Palm Springs.

We were missing them; we'd lived in close proximity and had the pleasure of their company often, with never more than a couple of weeks between precious visits. We had a nagging worry; Mom, who had been unwell, had endured a battery of tests the results of which were as yet unknown. She hoped that the prescription would be warm sunshine, rest and relaxation.

The test results came a few weeks later. Mom's doctor was known for his empathy and compassion; treating his patients, not their illness. When he couldn't reach her, he called us and caringly shared the painful reality; Multiple Myeloma, cancer of the white blood cells produced in the bone marrow, limited treatment options, and the hope of a cure, remote. We were reeling with the gravity of the situation, unsure of what we should do. Her doctor advised us to go to Palm Springs and assess Mom. If she was not well, accompany her quickly home and if she seemed alright, let her enjoy her time there. The proposed treatment could wait until she returned, the prognosis was not good.

A family trip to Palm Springs was almost ludicrous at this point in our professional lives. Two fresh new teachers, a new baby to provide with the required, "baby things", a pile of student loans, first home and car loans; to say finances were tight was an understatement! With a credit card in hand, we capitalized on the ten day Christmas school break and were off. Our deep love for our parents would always over-ride financial concerns.

I smile in retrospect; we were a couple of brave, or rather naïve twenty-one year old inexperienced tourists, from rural Saskatchewan, with a babe in tow. Feature us, in a rented car, heading off from L.A. airport at night, down unfamiliar freeways, bent on finding Palm Springs. We missed a few exits, hit a desert dead end, but finally rejoiced at our success in finding the R.V. Park. We approached the door with not a small amount of trepidation and some tears, wondering in what condition we would find them. My mom was gravely ill, yet I needed her, her love, her guidance, her motherly wisdom with our new child. This daughter and our future children would need their grandma. Thankfully, we would be together this Christmas.

We were amazed and delighted to be welcomed by this vibrant, tanned, seemingly healthy woman; my mother. She wrapped us all in warm and strong hugs. Our ten days together were wonderful and memorable; our daughter took her first steps in her grandparents' good company. They had planned an exciting side trip for us, a few days in Disneyland together, to add to this precious Christmas holiday.

Dad later disclosed that the trip south and the first few weeks for them had been trying and tough. Mom had been sore and weak, and spent most afternoons sleeping on a lounge in the therapeutic warm outdoors. She became stronger; they walked more, swam, and spent time laughing and enjoying the new friends they had made in the park.

Right or wrong, we chose not to share the doctor's diagnosis with them during our holiday. Mom seemed so content and happy. We knew there would be time for that, and we suspected a rough period lay ahead.

She returned home to Saskatchewan, in better shape than she had left, only to receive her dire diagnosis. She stoically endured a sometimes very unpleasant year of chemotherapy treatment and medical intervention.

The incredibly good news is that Mom lived to enjoy and grandparent our first daughter, our second daughter and our son into adulthood. She died of heart failure at the ripe age of 86. There are mysteries surrounding this dreaded illness. Mom's cancer was incurable and yet she seemed to have been cured. We rejoice and are grateful for the bonus years and Christmases which we celebrated with our beloved Mom and Grandma.

We are confident that someday the medical community will understand all the nuances of this disease.

Let's hope that will happen soon.

*"You don't choose your family, they are God's*
*gift to you, as you are to them."*
-Desmond Tutu

# Merry Christmas to All and to All a Good Diet!

Twas three months before Christmas, and all through the house,
Nothing would fit me, not even a blouse;
Appetizers I'd nibble, the cheesecake I'd taste,
And summer margaritas had gone to my waist;

When I got on the scale there arose such a number!
When I walked to the store (less a walk, more a lumber),
I'd remember the marvelous meals I'd prepared,
The gravies and sauces, no calories were spared.

The wine and the rum balls; the bread and the cheese,
and the way I'd never say, "No thank you, please."
As I dressed myself up in my husband's jean shirt,
and prepared once again to do battle with dirt,
I said to myself, as only I can,
"You can't spend a winter disguised as a man!"

So, away with the last of the sour cream dip.
Get rid of the chocolate cake, every cracker and chip.
Every last bit of food that I like must be banished,
'Til all the additional ounces have vanished.

I won't have a cookie--not even a lick.
I will only chew on a long celery stick.
I won't have hot biscuits, or corn bread, or pie,
I'll munch on a carrot and quietly cry.

I'm hungry, I'm lonesome, and life is a bore,
But isn't that what willpower is for?
Unable to giggle, no longer a riot.
Happy Christmas to all and to all a good diet!

# Sweet Treats for Santa

"Christmas may be a day of feasting, or
of prayer, but always it will be a day of
remembrance - a day in which we think
of everything we have ever loved."

- Augusta E. Rundel

# ALMOND FUDGE SHORTBREAD
## (Holiday tray worthy)

1 cup butter, softened
½ cup icing sugar
¼ teaspoon salt
1 ¼ cups flour
1 can sweetened condensed milk
2 cups semi-sweet chocolate chips
½ teaspoon almond extract
1/3 cup sliced almonds, toasted

In a bowl: cream butter, sugar and salt until fluffy. Gradually beat in flour. Spread into a greased 9 x 9 inch pan. Bake at 350° F. for about 18 minutes or until lightly browned. In a microwave-safe bowl, combine milk and chocolate chips. Microwave uncovered on high for 1-2 minutes or until chips are melted, stir until smooth. Stir in almond extract. Spread mixture over the shortbread, sprinkle with almonds and press down. Refrigerate until firm. Cut into small squares.

*"All we see of someone at any moment is a snapshot of their life, there in riches or poverty, in joy or despair. Snapshots don't show the million decisions that led to that moment."*
*- Richard Bach*

# ALMOND TOFFEE SQUARES
## (Easy and oh so yummy!)

1 cup butter
½ cup brown sugar
1 teaspoon vanilla
2 cups flour

Cream butter and sugar. Add vanilla. Mix in flour. Press into an ungreased 9 x 13 inch pan.
Bake at 350° F. for 15 minutes. Cool.

1 cup butter
½ cup brown sugar
2 teaspoons corn syrup
1 can sweetened condensed milk
½ cup slivered almonds

Boil butter, sugar, syrup and milk in microwave for 5 minutes in a large bowl. Stir after each minute. Pour over base and sprinkle with almonds. Cool. Freezes well.

**I understand the concept of cooking,
just not as it applies to me.**

# BAKLAVA

1 -450 gram package of frozen phyllo dough (20 sheets)

3 ½ cups walnuts, chopped

¼ cup fresh, fine breadcrumbs

1/3 cup sugar

1 teaspoon ground cinnamon

½ teaspoon ground cloves

1 cup plus 2 tablespoons butter, melted

Syrup:

1 cup sugar

1 cup water

5 tablespoons honey

juice and grated zest of 1 lemon

Thaw phyllo dough. To prevent drying keep covered with a slightly damp cloth or plastic wrap until used. Lightly butter a 9 x 13 inch baking pan; set aside. In a large bowl combine nuts, breadcrumbs, sugar, cinnamon and cloves. Preheat oven to 350° F. Place one phyllo sheet in buttered pan, folding it to fit pan. Lightly brush with melted butter. Repeat with five more phyllo sheets. Spread about one cup nut mixture; cover with 3 more phyllo sheets, brushing each with melted butter. Top with one cup nut mixture, then three more sheets, again brushing with butter. Repeat layers until nut mixture is gone. After layering final cup of nut mixture, layer five sheets of phyllo, buttering as before. Brush any remaining butter over the top sheet. Use a sharp knife and score top layers of phyllo in diamond pattern. Bake 40-50 minutes or until golden brown.

Continued on next page..................

**BAKLAVA** continued .................

<u>Syrup</u>: In a small saucepan, combine sugar, water, honey, lemon juice and zest. Bring to a boil and boil 10 minutes. Pour hot syrup evenly over top of baked baklava as soon as it comes from oven. Cool to room temperature and cut through remaining layers, following scoring. Makes about 24 pieces.

## FAVOURITE POUND CAKE
(This cake is wonderful with fruit, or for trifle,
or just as a yummy cake with tea!)

1 cup butter
3 cups sugar
1 cup sour cream
3 cups flour
½ teaspoon baking soda
6 eggs
1 teaspoon vanilla

Preheat oven to 325° F. Cream butter and sugar together; add sour cream. Sift flour and baking soda together. Add to creamed mixture, alternately with eggs, one at a time, beating after each. Add vanilla. Pour into a greased and floured tube pan and bake for 1 hour and 20 minutes.

"Did you ever notice that life seems to follow certain patterns?
I notice every year about this time, I hear Christmas music."
- Tom Sims

# BEST SECRET BROWNIES
## (The best brownies you will ever taste!)

4 squares unsweetened chocolate
¾ cup butter
2 cups sugar
3 large eggs
1 teaspoon vanilla
1 cup flour
1 cup pecans, chopped
2 Aero bars, crumbled

Preheat oven to 350° F. Place chocolate and butter in microwave safe bowl and microwave on high for 2-3 minutes, mixing periodically until melted. Add sugar, then mix in eggs and vanilla until well blended. Stir in flour. Add pecans and Aero bars and mix again. Pour mixture into a greased 9 x 9 inch pan and bake for about 40 minutes. Ice with your favourite icing while hot.

"Christmas is a time when you get homesick,
even when you're home."
– Carol Nelson

"Faith is that voice in the back of your
head that tells you to listen to that voice
in the back of your head."
- Dennis Miller

# CHERRY ALMOND NANAIMO BARS
## (A pretty, triple-layered bar. Freezes well.)

Bottom Layer:
½ cup butter
¼ cup sugar
1/3 cup cocoa
1 teaspoon vanilla
1 egg, beaten
1 cup flaked coconut
1 ¾ cups graham wafer crumbs
½ cup almonds, chopped

Filling:
¼ cup butter, softened
2 tablespoons cherry juice
1 teaspoon almond extract
2 cups icing sugar
1/3 cup maraschino cherries,
    chopped

Top Layer:
2 squares semi-sweet chocolate
1 tablespoon butter

Bottom Layer:  Cook butter, sugar, cocoa, vanilla and egg in a saucepan over low heat, stirring constantly, until mixture begins to thicken.  Remove from heat and stir in coconut, crumbs and almonds.  Pat firmly into a greased 9 inch square cake pan. Chill for at least one hour.
Filling:  Cream butter, cherry juice and almond extract. Gradually beat in icing sugar to make a smooth spreading consistency.  Stir in cherries.  Spread over first layer in pan. Chill until firm.
Top Layer:  Heat chocolate and butter in microwave, stirring often until smoothly melted.  Drizzle chocolate over filling.  Chill. Makes about 30 bars.

# CHRISTMAS EGGNOG CAKE
(There is no eggnog in the cake, but the finished cake tastes like Christmas eggnog.)

1 yellow cake mix
1 teaspoon ground nutmeg
¼ teaspoon ground ginger

Frosting:
1 ½ cups whipping/heavy cream
3 tablespoons icing sugar
1 teaspoon rum extract

Prepare cake according to package directions, adding spices. Bake at 350° F. for 25-30 minutes or until a toothpick comes out clean. Cool. In a small bowl, beat cream and icing sugar until stiff peaks form. Fold in extract. Spread over cake. Store in refrigerator.

*People will forget what you said.*
*People will forget what you did.*
*But people will never forget how you made them feel.*

# DELUXE FRUIT CAKE
## (Moist and simply delicious!)

1 -227 gram container red candied cherries
1 -227 gram container green candied cherries
1 -227 gram container citron peel
1 -227 gram container mixed peel
1 -454 gram package dark raisins
1 -908 gram package light raisins
1 -454 gram package currants
1 -454 gram package walnuts, chopped
4 cups flour
1 teaspoon mace
½ teaspoon ground cinnamon
½ teaspoon baking soda
½ pound butter
2 cups brown sugar
2 cups sugar
10 large eggs
1 -540 ml can crushed pineapple, drained and keep juice
1 teaspoon vanilla

Prepare fruit: wash and dry raisins and currants, and cut up cherries. Mix all fruit (except pineapple) and nuts in a large bowl. Pour pineapple juice over fruit and mix well.

Continued on next page........

# DELUXE FRUIT CAKE continued......

Sift flour, mace, ground cinnamon and baking soda.
Add flour mixture to fruit and mix until all fruit is coated with
flour. Cream butter and brown sugar until light and fluffy, add
white sugar and beat well. Add eggs 1 at a time, beating well
after each egg. Add pineapple and vanilla and beat until light.
Slowly add egg mixture to fruit mixture. Mix thoroughly.
Line 4 loaf pans with parchment paper and grease.
Place a pan of water in oven during baking.
Bake at 275° F. (no higher) for about 3 hours until toothpick
comes out clean.

"The odds of going to the store for a loaf
of bread and coming out with only a
loaf of bread are three billion to one."
-Erma Bombeck

"Grandma always made you feel she had been waiting to see
just you all day and now the day was complete."
- Marcy De Maree

# ARLENE'S LEMON DELIGHTS
### (These were Dragon, Arlene's favourite!)

2 cups flour

1 cup butter

1/3 cup whipping/heavy cream

½ cup sugar, divided

1 teaspoon lemon zest

1/8 teaspoon lemon extract

Combine flour, butter, cream, ¼ cup sugar, lemon zest and lemon extract in a large bowl. Mix on medium speed for 2 minutes, or until well blended. Divide dough into thirds, wrap in waxed paper and refrigerate until firm.

Place remaining ¼ cup of sugar in a shallow bowl. Roll each portion of dough thinly on well floured surface. Cut out dough with the cookie cutter of your choice. Dip both sides of each cookie in sugar and place 1 inch apart on greased cookie sheet. Pierce with a fork. Bake at 375° F. for 6-9 minutes, until cookies are slightly puffed, but not brown. Cool on cookie sheets for 1 minute, before transferring to wire rack.

Filling:

¾ cup icing sugar

¼ cup butter

3 teaspoons lemon juice

1 teaspoon vanilla

Combine and beat until smooth. Spread ½ teaspoon of filling on bottom half of cookies. Top with remaining cookies.

# BLITZEN'S BLUEBERRY BITES
## (Hearty and healthy for all of Santa's helpers)

½ cup butter

½ cup brown sugar

¼ cup white sugar

2 eggs

2 tablespoons water

1 teaspoon vanilla

¾ cup whole wheat flour

¾ teaspoon baking soda

¼ teaspoon salt

2 ½ cups rolled oats

1 cup ground flax

1 cup dried blueberries


Cream butter, beat in sugars. Add eggs, water and vanilla.
In a separate bowl, combine flour with baking soda and salt, add
to creamed mixture. Add rolled oats and flax, stir into batter.
Mix in blueberries. Using 1 tablespoon batter for each cookie;
roll into ball, place on lightly greased cookie sheet, and press
lightly down with a fork. Bake in 350° F. oven for
9-12 minutes. Cool on racks. Yield: about 50 cookies

"Christmas, children, is not a date. It is a state of mind."

- Mary Ellen Chase

# CHRISTMAS CHERROONS
## (A luscious variation to the crunchy macaroon!)

3 egg whites
¾ cup sugar
½ teaspoon salt
1 teaspoon almond extract
2 cups cornflakes
1 cup shredded coconut
½ cup mixed red and green cherries, slivered

Preheat oven to 350° F. In a large bowl beat egg whites until stiff and light. Fold in sugar and salt, gradually add extract. Fold in cornflakes, coconut and cherries. Drop from a small spoon onto greased cookie sheet. Bake on the middle rack for 10-12 minutes. Makes about 4 dozen cookies.

*"I like nonsense; it wakes up the brain cells.*
*Fantasy is a necessary ingredient on living;*
*it's a way of looking at life through the wrong end*
*of a telescope. Which is what I do, and that*
*enables you to laugh as life's realities."*
*- Dr. Seuss*

# CINNAMON LOGS

4 cups flour
½ cup sugar
2 cups butter or margarine
4 tablespoons ground cinnamon
½ cup brown sugar
¼ teaspoon salt

Mix all together. Shape into finger length logs or any other shape.
Bake at 350° F. for 10-15 minutes.

1 ½ teaspoons ground cinnamon
½ cup sugar

Combine cinnamon and sugar.
Roll logs in mixture while cookies are still warm.

"I refuse to spend my life worrying about what I eat. There's no pleasure worth foregoing just for an extra 3 years in the geriatric ward."
- John Mortimer

# COSTA RICAN ALMOND CHRISTMAS COOKIES

1 cup butter
½ cup sugar
1 ¾ cups flour
1 teaspoon salt
1 tablespoon almond extract
¾ cup almonds, chopped
icing sugar to dust cookies

Preheat oven to 350° F.
Beat butter and add sugar until creamy. Add flour and salt.
Mix well. Add almond extract and almonds. Shape into little
balls approximately ½ teaspoon each. Bake on lightly greased
cookie sheet for 12 min. Once the cookies have cooled, dust with
icing sugar.
Helpful Hint: Put icing sugar and cookies in ziplock bag and
shake gently until well covered.


"Our hearts grow tender with childhood memories and love of
kindred, and we are better throughout the year for having,
in spirit, become a child again at Christmas-time."
-Laura Ingalls Wilder

# DASHER'S GRANOLA DROPS
(Great for a midnight snack, keep the healthy side a secret.)

½ cup butter

½ cup brown sugar

2 eggs

¼ cup molasses

1 teaspoon vanilla

1 cup applesauce

1 ½ cups flour

½ teaspoon baking soda

½ teaspoon salt

½ cup powdered milk

1 ½ cups rolled oats

¾ cup coconut

¾ cup wheat germ

¾ cup sunflower seeds

1 cup dried fruit (cranberries, blueberries, or raisins work well)

1/3 cup sesame seeds

1 cup chocolate chips

1 cup walnuts or almonds, chopped (optional)

Cream together; butter, brown sugar, eggs, molasses, and vanilla. Stir in applesauce. In a separate bowl mix flour, baking soda, salt and powdered milk. Add powdered mixture to wet ingredients, blend well. Add remaining ingredients, mix well. Drop from tablespoon on greased cookie sheet, or roll in floured hands. Bake at 350° F. for 12-15 minutes. These freeze well.

# DRAGON'S DEN COOKIES
## (These were a hit with the Dragons.)

1 cup butter

1 cup sugar

1 egg

pinch of salt

2 teaspoons ground cinnamon

1 teaspoon vanilla

2 cups flour

Cream butter and sugar. Add remaining ingredients. Roll into small balls, as this is a sweet rich cookie. Place on a greased cookie sheet. Flatten cookies with floured fork to give waffle appearance (the flatter, the better).
Bake at 350° F. for 8-12 minutes.

Filling:

½ cup butter

½ cup brown sugar

1 teaspoon ground cinnamon

¼ cup corn syrup

Mix in saucepan. Heat until brown sugar is dissolved. Cool, then spread between cookies. Enjoy!
These are a decadent cookie commonly served with tea; place the cookie on the cup to warm the delicious filling.

<u>Shown on previous page:</u>

Stained-Glass Cookies — Page 190
Meringue Mushrooms — Page 201
Chocolate Yule Log — Page 143
Homemade Turtles — Page 200
Santa's Whiskers — Page 188
Rosettes — Page 194
Arlene's Lemon Delights — Page 180
Almond Fudge Shortbread — Page 171
Christmas Cherroons — Page 182
White Chocolate Macadamia Cookies — Page 192
Christmas Mice — Page 195

# PEANUT BUTTER CUP COOKIES

1 ¾ cups flour
½ teaspoon salt
1 teaspoon baking soda
½ cup butter, softened
½ cup sugar
½ cup peanut butter
½ cup brown sugar, packed
1 egg, beaten
1 teaspoon vanilla
2 tablespoons milk
40 miniature chocolate covered peanut butter cups

Preheat oven to 375° F. Sift together: flour, salt and baking soda; set aside. Cream together: butter, sugar, peanut butte and brown sugar until fluffy. Beat in egg, vanilla and milk. Add flour mixture; mix well. Shape into 40 balls and place each into an ungreased mini muffin pan. Bake at 375° F. for about 8 minutes. Remove from oven and immediately press a mini peanut butter cup into each ball. Cool and carefully remove from pan.

**Definition of a teenager?**
**God's punishment...for enjoying sex.**

# SANTA'S WHISKERS

1 cup butter, softened
1 cup sugar
2 eggs
1 teaspoon baking powder
1 teaspoon rum extract
3 ¼ cups flour
¾ cup red and green mixed candied cherries, chopped
½ cup pecans, chopped
½ cup coconut

Combine first 6 ingredients, mix well. Add cherries and pecans.
Divide into 2 halves and form each into a 2 inch diameter roll.
Roll each roll in coconut and wrap in wax paper and chill.
Slice ¼ inch wide and place on ungreased cookie sheet.
Bake at 350° F. for 10-12 minutes.

*"Some people weave burlap into the fabric of our lives,*
*and some weave gold thread.*
*Both contribute to make the whole*
*picture to make it beautiful and unique."*
*- Anonymous*

# SOFT & CHEWY CHOCOLATE COOKIES

4 tablespoons butter
1 cup semi-sweet chocolate chips
¾ cup flour
½ teaspoon baking powder
½ teaspoon salt
2 large eggs
¾ cup brown sugar
1 teaspoon vanilla
2 cups semi-sweet chocolate chips

Preheat oven to 350° F. Heat butter and 1 cup chocolate chips in microwave for 20 second increments, stirring in between until almost melted. Do not overheat. In another bowl, whisk flour, baking powder and salt. In a mixing bowl; beat eggs, brown sugar and vanilla on high speed until light and fluffy. Reduce speed, add melted chocolate. Mix in flour mixture until just combined. Stir in chocolate chips. Drop by heaping tablespoons of dough 2-3 inches apart onto greased baking sheets. Bake, rotating baking sheets halfway through, until cookies are shiny and crackly yet soft in centres, about 12-15 minutes. Cool on sheets for 10 minutes.

"May Peace be your gift at Christmas
and your blessing all year through!"
-Author Unknown

189

# STAINED GLASS COOKIES

(Kids love to hang these on the tree as a treat not
only for Santa, but for themselves as well!)

1 cup sugar
½ cup butter, softened
1/3 cup vegetable shortening
2 eggs
1 teaspoon orange zest, grated
1 teaspoon vanilla
2 ¾ cups flour
1 teaspoon baking powder
1 teaspoon salt
5 rolls life saver candies, assorted flavours

In large bowl combine sugar, butter and shortening. Beat at
medium speed until light and fluffy. Add eggs, zest and vanilla.
Beat at medium speed until well blended. Add flour, baking
powder and salt. Beat at low speed until soft dough forms.
Cover with plastic wrap. Chill 1-2 hours, or until firm.

Line cookie sheets with foil. Divide dough into thirds. On well
floured surface, roll 1/3 of the dough to ¼ inch thickness. Using
3 inch cookie cutters, cut desired shapes into dough. Place
shapes 2 inches apart on prepared cookie sheets.

Continued on next page........

# STAINED GLASS COOKIES continued.....

Using smaller cookie cutters, straws or a sharp knife, cut desired shapes out of cookies on cookie sheets. (If cookies are to be hung as ornaments, using a plastic straw, make a small hole at the top of each cookie for string.) Repeat with remaining dough.
Place like-coloured candies in small plastic bags. Coarsely crush candies by tapping each bag with back of a large spoon. Fill cut out areas of cookies to the top with candies. Bake in a 350° F. oven for 7-9 minutes, or until edges are light golden brown and candies are melted. Cool completely before removing from foil. Gently pull cookies off foil. Makes about 4 dozen cookies.

"At Christmas
A man is at his finest towards the finish of the year;
He is almost what he should be when the Christmas season's here;
Then he's thinking more of others than he's
thought the months before,
And the laughter of his children is a joy worth toiling for.
He is less a selfish creature than at any other time;
When the Christmas spirit rules him he comes
close to the sublime."
-Edgar Guest

# WHITE CHOCOLATE MACADAMIA COOKIES

½ cup butter, softened
½ cup shortening
¾ cup brown sugar
½ cup sugar
1 egg
1 ½ teaspoons vanilla
2 cups flour
1 teaspoon baking soda
½ teaspoon salt
3 squares white chocolate, cut into small chunks
1 -200 gram can macadamia nuts, coarsely chopped

Beat butter and shortening until soft and creamy. Gradually add sugars, beating well. Add egg and vanilla. Combine flour, baking soda, and salt; gradually add to butter mixture, and beat. Stir in white chocolate and nuts. Drop dough by rounded teaspoonfuls 2 inches apart onto lightly greased cookie sheet. Bake at 350° F. for 8-10 minutes, or until lightly browned. Makes 5 dozen.

*"People are like dynamite. The power is on the inside, but nothing happens until the fuse gets lit."*
*- Mac Anderson*

# CANDIED CHRISTMAS NUTS

500 grams walnut halves
1 cup sugar
  teaspoons ground cinnamon
¼ teaspoon salt
6 tablespoons milk
1 teaspoon vanilla

Preheat oven to 350° F. Spread nuts in a single layer on a baking sheet. Roast for approximately 8-10 minutes. Stir together; sugar, cinnamon, salt, and milk in a medium saucepan. Cook over medium-high heat for 8 minutes (or until the mixture reaches the soft ball stage of 236° F.) stirring constantly. Remove from heat, and stir in vanilla immediately. Add walnuts to syrup, and stir to coat well. Spoon nuts onto waxed paper, and immediately separate nuts with a fork. Cool and store in airtight containers.

Tell a man there are 300 billion stars in the
universe and he'll believe you.
Tell him a bench has wet paint on it,
and he'll have to touch it to be sure.
-Murphy's Law

# CARAMEL CORN
## (Make ahead and freeze, to keep fresh for a holiday treat.)

2 cups brown sugar

1 cup margarine

½ cup corn syrup

¼ teaspoon cream of tartar

12 cups popped popcorn

Mix brown sugar, margarine, corn syrup, and cream of tartar in a saucepan and boil for 7 minutes. Put popcorn in a large roaster. Pour sauce over popcorn and stir to coat. Bake at 200° F. for 2 hours, stirring frequently, until popcorn is dry.

# ROSETTES
## (A special treat at Christmas time!)

2 eggs, slightly beaten

2 tablespoons sugar

1 cup milk

1 cup flour

¼ teaspoon salt

1 tablespoon lemon extract

oil for frying

Add sugar to eggs, and then stir in milk. Sift flour before measuring, then sift together again with salt. Stir flour into egg mixture and beat until smooth. Add lemon extract. Allow batter to sit 2 hours in fridge before frying. Deep fry as directed with rosette iron. Sprinkle with icing sugar or cinnamon and sugar.

# CHRISTMAS MICE

(These are fun to make with children and they look so nice
on a Christmas baking tray; they taste good too.)

1 ½ cups chocolate melting wafers
24 red maraschino cherries with stems, well drained
24 milk chocolate kisses
48 sliced almonds
1 tube red decorating gel
1 tube white decorating gel or 48 small white candy dots

In a saucepan over low heat, melt chocolate wafers and stir until
smooth. Make sure cherry is quite dry, and holding each cherry
by the stem, dip in melted chocolate, then press onto the bottom
of a chocolate kiss. For ears, place almonds between the cherry
and kiss. Refrigerate until set. With white gel or candy dots
apply eyes and with red gel, pipe a nose on the tip of the
chocolate kiss. Store in an airtight container at room
temperature.


"As an adult I find it difficult to sleep on Christmas Eve.
Yuletide excitement is a potent caffeine, no matter your age."
-Carrie Latet

# CREAM CHRISTMAS CANDIES
### (Makes a last minute, tasty colorful addition to candy trays)

½ cup cream cheese, softened
¼ teaspoon peppermint or almond extract
3 cups icing sugar
green and red coloured sugar (optional)

In a small mixing bowl combine cream cheese and extract. Beat
in 1 ½ cups icing sugar. Knead in remaining sugar until smooth.
Shape into ½ inch balls. Roll in coloured sugar if desired.
(Green with peppermint, and red with almond flavouring is
nice.)
Place on ungreased surface and flatten with a fork. Let stand one
hour to harden. Store in an airtight container in the refrigerator.
Makes about 6 dozen.

*"As a rule, what is out of sight disturbs men's minds
more seriously than what they see."*
*- Julius Caesar*

# EGGNOG CHOCOLATE FUDGE

2 cans sweetened condensed milk
1 -340 gram package bittersweet chocolate chips
3 cups white chocolate chips
1 ½ teaspoons rum extract
½ teaspoon vanilla
½ teaspoon ground nutmeg
1/8 teaspoon salt

Line an 8 inch square baking pan with enough foil to overhang edges by 2 inches. Coat with cooking spray. Pour condensed milk into a large microwave safe bowl. Add bittersweet chocolate chips and microwave on high for 30 second intervals, stirring until smooth. Pour mixture into cake pan.
Pour remaining can of milk into another microwave safe bowl and add white chocolate chips. Microwave on high for 30 second intervals, stirring until smooth. Add extracts, nutmeg and salt. Gently spread mixture over the first layer in pan. Refrigerate until set (6-8 hours). Using foil, lift fudge from pan and cut into squares. Garnish with dragées or chocolate shavings. Note: This freezes well. Wrap in plastic and foil.

**I find it helps to divide chores into categories;
things I won't do now,
things I won't do later
and things I will never do.**

# HOLIDAY DIVINITY CANDY

2 cups sugar

½ cup water

1/3 cup light corn syrup

2 egg whites

1 teaspoon vanilla

1/8 teaspoon salt

¼ cup candied cherries, diced

¼ cup candied pineapple, diced

1 cup walnuts, chopped

In a heavy saucepan, combine sugar, water and corn syrup; cook and stir until sugar is dissolved and mixture comes to a boil. Cook over medium heat, without stirring, until a candy thermometer reads 250° F. (hard-ball stage). Remove from heat. In a mixing bowl, beat egg whites until stiff peaks form. Slowly pour hot sugar mixture over egg whites, beating constantly. Add vanilla and salt. Beat until candy loses its gloss and holds its shape, about 14 minutes. Stir in fruit and nuts. Drop by teaspoonfuls onto waxed paper.

"Christmas is the season when you buy this year's gifts
with next year's money."
~Author Unknown

# HOMEMADE TURKISH DELIGHT
## (This is the best Turkish delight ever!)

1 can jellied cranberry sauce
1 cup sugar
3 small boxes strawberry jelly powder
1 -88 ml pouch liquid fruit pectin
2 cups chocolate melting wafers (optional)

Line a 9 x 13 inch baking pan with non-stick aluminum foil, non-stick side up, letting the foil extend for several inches on both sides of the baking pan.  In a medium saucepan, heat cranberry sauce over medium heat whisking vigorously. Once sauce is smooth; whisk in sugar and jello powder. Bring to a full boil scraping down sides of sauce pan with a rubber spatula. Reduce heat to medium low and maintain a gentle boil for 8 minutes, stirring often.  Remove from heat and stir in pectin until sauce is well blended. Pour mixture into pan and spread evenly. Refrigerate overnight or until jelly is very firm. Lift jelly from pan by foil edges and loosen edges with a small knife. Cut into 1 inch squares. Melt the chocolate wafers over low heat until liquid. Dip each square into chocolate and set on a rack or wax paper to dry and set. *You may just dust the Turkish delight with icing sugar rather than dip in chocolate.
Hint: Hide these or there will be none left for Christmas.

# HOMEMADE TURTLES

Base:

4-5 cups pecans, lightly toasted

Line 2 cookie sheets with parchment paper. Set toasted pecans in groups of threes on cookie sheets, then set aside.

(About 7 dozen groupings)

Caramel:

| | |
|---|---|
| 1 cup sugar | 1 cup corn syrup |
| 1 cup butter | 1 can sweetened condensed milk |

In a medium saucepan combine sugar, corn syrup and butter. Bring to a boil over medium heat, stirring constantly. Simmer slowly for 4 minutes without stirring. Remove from heat and stir in condensed milk. Reduce heat to medium low and cook until caramel is at softball stage, stirring constantly, as it will burn easily. (It will thicken slightly and turn a more golden brown.) Remove from heat; scoop warm caramel by teaspoonful and drop on each group of pecans. Cool completely.

Coating:

1 kg good quality chocolate

Melt chocolate over low heat and remove from heat as soon as chocolate is melted. If chocolate is too hot it will slip off turtles and pool around the bottom. When caramel is cool dip "naked" turtles into melted chocolate and set back on cookie sheet. Pop dipped turtles in freezer for a couple of minutes to set chocolate. Store turtles in a sealed container in a cool place. Do not freeze; do not store in the fridge.

# MERINGUE MUSHROOMS
(These are the first to go off our cookie trays at Christmas, and they are wonderful for gift giving.)

2 large egg whites, room temperature
¼ teaspoon cream of tartar
½ cup sugar
½ cup semi-sweet chocolate chips

Preheat oven to 225° F. Line 2 cookie sheets with parchment paper or aluminum foil. In a large glass or metal bowl, use an electric mixer to whip egg whites until foamy. Add cream of tartar and continue whipping, until whites hold soft peaks. Gradually sprinkle in sugar, so that it does not sink to bottom, and continue whipping until mixture holds stiff shiny peaks. Using a pastry bag and round tip, squeeze out round mounds of meringue onto one of prepared cookie sheets for mushroom caps. Pull bag off to side to avoid making peaks on top. For stems, press out a small circle of meringue onto other sheet, then pull bag straight up. The mushrooms will look more natural if pieces are not all perfect. Dust mushroom caps lightly with cocoa using a small sifter. Bake for 1 hour, or until caps are dry enough to easily remove from cookie sheets. Set aside to cool completely. Melt chocolate carefully over low heat. Poke a small hole in bottom of a mushroom cap. Spread chocolate over bottom of cap. Dip tip of a stem in chocolate, and press lightly into hole. When chocolate sets, they will hold together. Store at room temperature in a dry place or tin.

# MICROWAVE TOFFEE

1 cup butter
1 can sweetened condensed milk
1 cup brown sugar
5 tablespoons corn syrup

Be sure to use a large bowl as this mixture boils over easily.
Melt butter in microwave. Add remaining ingredients and
microwave until it bubbles (about 3 minutes). Boil an additional
12 minutes in microwave on medium to high setting, stirring
every 3 minutes. Pour into a greased 9 x 13 inch pan. Cool
and cut. This freezes well.

# CRANBERRY MACADAMIA BARK

500 grams white chocolate dipping wafers
1 cup macadamia nuts
½ cup dried cranberries

In a saucepan, melt chocolate over medium-low heat, stirring
until smooth. Add nuts and cranberries; mix well. Spread onto a
foil-lined baking sheet. Cool. Break into pieces.

*"I take a simple view of life:*
*keep your eyes open and get on with it."*
*- Sir Laurence Olivier*

# RUM BALLS

2 squares semi-sweet chocolate
½ cup cream cheese
¼ cup corn syrup
1/3 cup rum
¼ cup icing sugar
2 cups chocolate Oreo wafers, crushed
crushed pecans (optional)
chocolate sprinkles (optional)
colored sprinkles (optional)

Melt chocolate, and mix in cheese, syrup and rum. Add icing sugar and wafers. Refrigerate 2 hours. Roll into balls and roll in any of the optional coverings.


"It is the one season of the year when we can lay aside all gnawing worry, indulge in sentiment without censure, assume the carefree faith of childhood, and just plain "have fun." Whether they call it Yuletide, Noel, Weinachten, or Christmas, people around the earth thirst for its refreshment as the desert traveller for the oasis."
-D.D. Monroe

# SENSATIONAL TRUFFLES

1 -250 gram package cream cheese, softened
8 squares semi-sweet chocolate, melted
1 cup of each white and dark chocolate wafers

Mix cream cheese and chocolate. Refrigerate 1 hour. Shape
into 36 balls. Melt chocolate wafers, separately in microwave
oven, one minute at a time until melted. Using toothpicks, dip
half the cheese balls into each mixture. Place on tray and
refrigerate an additional hour. Store in an air-tight container.

Variations:
Add ¾ cup Skor bits to cheese instead of melted chocolate.
Just leave them plain without chocolate.
Decorate each coated ball with sprinkles.
Roll balls in powdered cocoa.

"Oh, for the good old days when people would stop
Christmas shopping when they ran out of money."
-Author Unknown

# SNOW TOFFEE

(This is a fun tradition to share with grandchildren.
They look so forward to it every year. Mine once told me that if
I could sell this toffee I would make a million dollars, because no
other candy tastes so good — I think it is just because it is eaten
outside in the snow and it is made with Grandma's love!)

1 can sweetened condensed milk
1 cup butter (not margarine)
½ cup corn syrup
2 cups brown sugar

Mix all ingredients in a large saucepan. Cook over medium
heat, stirring frequently until mixture comes to a gentle boil.
Stir and boil for about 8 minutes. Remove from heat.
Find a nice clean patch of snow outside and let each child choose
their area. Drizzle the toffee from the pot into lines in the snow
in front of each child. (Be careful as you are dealing with a hot
syrupy, burning, liquid and children must not touch, until it hits
the snow and sets.) After it sits in the snow for a minute or two
let the child gather it up in a ball and form it around a spoon or
popsicle stick to enjoy.
*I often give the kids a glass and spoon in case their wrapping
job isn't too secure, they can plop the toffee into a glass and eat
it that way. This recipe easily gives a dozen children a nice
lollipop size of toffee with some left over in the pot for the adults
to spoon out and enjoy! It will never set into a hard crack toffee,
so not much use spreading it into a pan! Just enjoy from the pot!

## Paige's Christmas Wish
### (an excerpt from Paige's story)

This will be my last blog as Christmas is right around the corner. I spent one Christmas and New Years at BC Children's Hospital so my thoughts and heart are with all the children in hospital this Christmas season. I live my life with hope in my heart. Hope for a world where all children can play. Hope for a world where children are not robbed of their childhoods. Hope for a world where children and adults alike no longer fear the word cancer. Hope for a world where cancer no longer exists. I guess that is my Christmas wish this year.   Love Paige

Paige has a blog online through the B.C. Children's Hospital – we were given permission to reprint this excerpt from Paige.

*I leave everything to the last possible moment - a procrastinator through and through. I don't like it, but it is who I am. Christmas 2005, found me once again, leaving Christmas shopping until I was finished work on the 20th of December. On the 18th I had a mammogram that showed a lump and within hours I was talking to a surgeon who told me it looked like cancer, and surgery was scheduled for Dec 22. Shopping was on the bottom of my list of to do's. After my surgery, I was told that it was cancer and that they couldn't get it all.*

*I was still in the hospital on December 23 and decided I could dwell on my plight, or send my four children shopping. They took every credit card and debit card I owned and went shopping. Now to be honest, there weren't unlimited resources, but those four teenagers made sure that there were gifts for everyone.*

*Opening them Christmas morning, we laughed and laughed at the variety of presents, the duplicates-the four pair of pants for one of them. The youngest of the four was thirteen and he commented on the number of gifts. I received a curling iron and hair products and we laughed again because we knew in a few months I would be bald! It could have been the worst Christmas of our lives, the future was so uncertain, but we didn't set cancer a place at the table. We celebrated, we laughed, we ate, and we had fun!*

*"Life can turn on a dime, the direction you head in, when it does, makes all the difference"*
*- Barbara Delinsky*

207

# NEW YEAR'S WISHES

*May you get a clean bill of health from your dentist, your cardiologist, your gastro-endocrinologist, your urologist, your proctologist, your podiatrist, your psychiatrist, your gynecologist, your plumber and Revenue Canada.*

*May your hair, your teeth, your face-lift, your abs and your stocks not fall; and may your blood pressure, your triglycerides, your cholesterol, your white blood count and your mortgage interest not rise.*

*May you find a way to travel from anywhere to anywhere in the rush hour in less than an hour, and when you get there may you find a parking space.*

*May December 31, find you seated around the dinner table, together with your beloved family or cherished friends, ushering in the new year ahead. You will find the food better, the environment quieter, the cost much cheaper, and the pleasure much more fulfilling than anything else you might ordinarily do that night.*

*May you wake up on January 1st, and what you see in the mirror delight you, and what others see in you delight them.*

*May someone love you enough to forgive your faults, be blind to your blemishes, and tell the world about your virtues.*

*May the telemarketers wait to make their sales calls until you finish dinner, and may your cheque book and your budget balance and may they include generous amounts for charity.*

*May you remember to say "I love you" or better yet show, "I love you" to your spouse, your child, your parents, your friends; but not to your secretary, your nurse, your masseuse, your hairdresser or your tennis instructor.*

*May we live as our maker intended, in a world at peace and the awareness of His love in every sunset, every flower's unfolding petals, every baby's smile, every lover's kiss, and every wonderful, astonishing, miraculous beat of our heart.*

### *A Very Happy New Year to All!*

# HOLLY JOLLY APPETIZERS AND BEVERAGES

# CHRISTMAS MORNING BRUNCHES AND BREADS

## FESTIVE CHRISTMAS DINNERS

## SEASONAL SALADS AND SIDE DISHES

## JOYOUS CHRISTMAS DESSERTS

## SWEET TREATS
## FOR SANTA

# Breast Friends Cookbooks

| For the Breasts of Friends<br>Cookbook 1 | For the Breasts and<br>the Rest of Friends | Breast Wishes<br>Cookbook 3 |
|:---:|:---:|:---:|
| 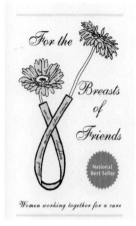 | 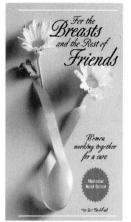 |  |
| | Cookbook 2 | |

## BREAST FRIENDS' CHRISTMAS RECOMMENDATIONS

| Recipe | Page | Cookbook |
|:---|:---:|:---:|
| Breakfast Lasagna | 53 | #3 |
| Candy Canes | 352 | #2 |
| Caroler's Potato Soup | 115 | #3 |
| Carrot Pudding & Rum Sauce | 250 | #1 |
| Celebration Cranberry Sauce | 235 | #3 |
| Celebration Never Fail Chiffon Cake | 308 | #2 |
| Chocolate Cinnamon Dessert | 281 | #2 |
| Chocolate Orange Truffles | 374 | #3 |
| Classic Chocolate Fudge | 382 | #2 |
| Coconut Cheese Ball | 5 | #1 |
| Cranberry Punch | 42 | #3 |
| Dilly Buns | 95 | #2 |
| Donna's Mandarin Orange Salad | 405 | #2 |

# A Gift of Hope
## Order Form - Breast Friends Cookbooks

<u>Please send:</u>    *prices include GST

___Book one **"For the Breasts of Friends"** @ 20.95 ___

___Book two **"For the Breasts and the Rest of Friends"** @ 20.95___

___Book three **"Breast Wishes"** @ 20.95 ___

___Book four **"Breast Wishes for Christmas"** @ $15.70 ___

Shipping and handling in Canada: Please enclose $6.30 for one book, $10.50 for 2 to 5 books, $15.75 for 5 to 10 books. (Includes GST) Over 10 books - call or email to make shipping arrangements. For out of country orders, please contact us by email or phone to order.

Total for books $_____ plus shipping $_____ = total enclosed _____

**Net profits from the sale of the books go to cancer agencies, patient needs, equipment and research.**
**See our website for examples of agencies that have received donations or sold our book for their cause.**

Name_____

Street or Box_____

City, Province_____

Country, Postal Code (Zip Code)_____

Make cheques payable to **Breast Friends**. Send order to Breast Friends, Box 436, Foam Lake, SK  S0A 1A0 The book can also be ordered by calling 1-877-560-4547 or by email at **breastfriends@sasktel.net.** The website **www.breastfriends.ca** features sample recipes, more information and an ordering link.